# *MESSAGES FROM SHIVA Vol. 1*

Channeled by River Lightbearer

In collaboration with Shiva, a being of light

This work is the sole intellectual property of Kimberly Ramsey-Winkler/River Lightbearer. It is available for personal use only. Digital versions cannot legally be loaned or given to others. The scanning or upload of this book for distribution is legally prohibited. No part of this book may be shared or reproduced without the express written permission of the author. To obtain permission, please contact the publisher at info@riverevolutions.com.

© 2021 Kimberly Ramsey-Winkler/River Lightbearer

Cover by Winterheart Design

Published by:

Vegan Wolf Productions
veganwolfproductions@gmail.com

# Contents

Intro: My "Invisible" Friends and I    1

Shiva's Introduction    9

Know Love    13

Know Yourself    20

Know Compassion    31

Know Trust    44

Know Power    56

Know Responsibility    64

Know Change    71

Know Balance    82

Know Connection    88

Shiva's Closing Message    99

Acknowledgements    101

## RIVER'S INTRODUCTION: MY "INVISIBLE FRIENDS" AND I

When I mention to people that I channel, they often have questions. A lot of questions.

Channeling isn't something that's well-known, especially in the mainstream, day-to-day society in which most of us pass our time. Even those who do know a little about channeling assume it's the same as mediumship (which is communication with dead spirits) or believe it's something that happens to you rather than something you choose to do. There are a number of misconceptions and misunderstandings about what channeling is, and there really isn't room for me to address all of them in what's meant to be a fairly short introduction to this book.

However, I'll give a little background about my experiences with my guides and with channeling, and hopefully I'll bring some insight by doing so.

My childhood wasn't the most pleasant or the most nurturing. I'm an only child. My father is also an only child and never quite saw the logic in socializing with others. My mother's family is in another country; she wasn't close with them, seemed to get very stuck on the "rules" of how to navigate interpersonal connections, and became a mother because that's what women were supposed to do.

Both of my parents worked outside the home, even though in the early 1970s that was uncommon, and they seemed at times to be alternately annoyed or exhausted by me. I realized when I was very young that I had to take care of myself, because the adults around me weren't doing as effective a job as I needed.

I didn't have many friends, because I didn't really understand how to behave with other children. I wasn't around other kids often anyway, and even when I was, I didn't understand why I couldn't talk about the things I saw or "just knew," or why kids thought I was weird or bossy when I was just being honest.

I was about two years old when my first two "invisible friends" first showed up in my life. I called them Big John and Little John, partly because of a TV show I watched that had characters by those names, and partly because...well, I was two. Names weren't my strong suit.

In my two-year-old mind, Big John was a teenager, strong and protective; Little John was a toddler, younger than me, not even able to speak yet. Big John took care of me, and Little John was my playmate. I loved them. I felt loved by them.

Over time, more invisible friends came to me. I talked to my parents and other adult relatives about them. The adults indulged me because I was an "imaginative child," and even the adults who otherwise found me difficult to deal with were respectful of creativity. They weren't entirely happy, though, when they referred to my "imaginary friends" and I vehemently corrected them. "They aren't imaginary! They're just invisible!"

When I was around four, my most powerful "invisible friend" arrived. He was extremely loving and protective. Any time he was with me, I felt warm, safe, and nurtured. I never had any doubt that he was abundantly *good*. My parents took me to church sometimes, and being raised in a nominally Christian environment, I could think of only one name that applied to this powerfully loving being: Jesus. In the privacy of my room, when my parents would send me to play alone, I pretended I was this being's daughter.

Spending most of my time isolated from other humans, I became extremely close to my invisible friends. And more and more showed up. By the time I was seven, there were around forty of them, each with their own name and personality. Not all of them were with me all the time; some just dropped by to visit periodically. The consistent ones were "Big John," "Little John," "Jesus," and two or three others.

Over time, I expected them to leave. According to my mother's women's magazines, which I started reading out of boredom when I was around eight, it was normal for children to have imaginary friends as preschoolers, but they outgrew those imaginary friends by or before the middle of elementary school. Even though I didn't want my friends to disappear, I knew I was growing up. Even though I knew they weren't imaginary, the "helpful" adults around me had convinced me to doubt that knowledge. So I assumed they would go away eventually.

While some of the occasional visitors stopped showing up, though, my consistent "invisible friends" didn't leave. Not only that, but as I got older, they talked to me about deeper subjects and how to navigate more painful situations in my life. They sometimes were playful and entertaining, and sometimes a little tough on me as they tried to teach me to embrace my inner power to create a positive life for myself. Never mean or pushy, though; they just didn't take excuses.

By the time I was around twelve, "Jesus" had stopped speaking with me, though I still felt his presence at times. The others remained. At that time, I knew them as Tom (formerly "Big John"), J, and Sim. A few years later, another, Shanise, made herself known.

One of my favorite stories about my "invisible friends," and the one I most often tell when someone asks me how I know they're real and not my imagination, is from my grade 11 Algebra class. I was failing that class. Math is worse than a foreign language to me; my brain, after a certain point, just hears nonsense. I had gone to the teacher for extra help after school more than once, and his response was to regurgitate exactly what he'd said in class. Since I hadn't understood it in class, I obviously wasn't going to understand it three hours later, but that didn't seem to register with him.

One day, we had a test over a chapter I hadn't understood at all. I had failed almost every homework assignment in that chapter and couldn't even begin to figure out how to solve the problems on the test. I was about to burst into tears when J said (in my mind's ear), "Just add those numbers."

"What?" It wasn't so much that I hadn't heard as that I couldn't believe what I was hearing.

"Just do what I tell you, and you'll do fine." And J proceeded to walk me through solving every problem on the test.

A few days later, when the tests were graded and returned, I'd gotten a B. On a test in a class where I'd consistently gotten D's and F's, over material of which I hadn't had even a slight understanding. Because one of my invisible—not imaginary—friends had helped.

Fast forward into adulthood. At age 34, I'd been in an abusive marriage for twelve years. I had two children whom I adored, but I was struggling to be the mother they needed me to be. My biggest escapes were reading and writing, and although my children's father did his best to prevent me from doing those things because he found them somehow offensive, I did them anyway.

Through it all, my "invisible friends" stayed with me,

supporting me during the difficult times with my husband, helping me try to find my footing as a mother, and all the while encouraging me to be my best self and know that things would get better. By this time, I knew better than to mention my friends to anyone, of course, but they gave me the support and solace I needed as I navigated my life.

In 2005, things started to change. Through a seemingly random chain of events—which were anything but random, of course—I became friends with a man who practiced energy healing and channeling. We bonded first over writing, as we were both writers who had yet to be published, but as our friendship progressed, he started teaching me about the skills he possessed. He was the one who first explained to me that my "invisible friends" were actually my guides, beings who had chosen to work with me in this lifetime and possibly others.

He also explained, partly through his knowledge and partly by asking his own guide about my situation, that my primary guide had "capped my channel." This meant that my primary guide had put energetic protections in place so that only my own guides could connect with and communicate with me. Other beings could try—and had tried over the years—to speak with me, but they could do so only if I gave permission and my primary guide opened the protections. This was done because I was so young when my guides first connected with me that I would have been in danger otherwise, and the protections had remained in place ever since.

I liked that. It helped me feel loved and safe, something I desperately needed.

My friend did energy healing sessions with me that brought to light many pieces of my past so I could begin the deeper work of healing from the abuse and traumas I'd experienced. He taught me the energy healing modality he used, and over time I became a Master Teacher in that modality, Chios® He also did channeling sessions with me in which he entered trance so I could speak directly to his guide, a being of light.

I was uncomfortable with my friend's guide, because the energetic vibration was so high and positive that I felt unworthy and "low" by comparison. But I also trusted my friend and his guide. When someone I knew was struggling with what appeared to be an energetic illness, my friend and his guide encouraged me, with the gifts and skills with which I'd learned to work, to be the one to help her. My friend said, "You should call on Shiva to help. I just feel like that's who you need to ask. He's a being of light, like my guide."

I really didn't feel "worthy" of calling on Shiva, but I trusted my friend, so I did. The energy work I did for my other friend was effective, and I felt so pleased with what I'd been able to do. That night, during my meditation as I was preparing to go to bed, I heard a voice in my mind say, "Well done, Ganatram." The next day, I told my friend about this, and he said that "Ganatram" was likely to be a spiritual name Shiva had chosen to give me.

A few days later, I came down with a bad cold. My friend said that if I would allow it, his guide could "innervate" me (his consciousness could enter my body) to clear out what appeared to be partly an energetic attack from the same situation that had sickened my other friend. I agreed, and my friend's guide and I did the innervation that night.

The illness cleared my system quickly after that, but that wasn't the only purpose. My friend's guide also restored the connections between Shiva and me. What I hadn't understood was that Shiva, the being of light, was the "invisible friend" I'd called Jesus when I was little.

Because of the traumas I'd experienced, my energetic vibration had dropped too low for Shiva to work with me directly without risking causing me harm; that was why he'd stopped speaking to me, though he had never left me. Now I'd done enough work toward healing the trauma that my vibration was in the safe range again, and with the help of my friend's guide, Shiva and I were able to connect and work together again.

With the connection restored, I learned to channel, first for myself and then for others. Learning to enter a trance state was easy for me; I had used self-hypnosis and dissociation without realizing it for most of my life to escape abuse and trauma. Learning to let my consciousness "step aside" so Shiva could innervate me and speak through me was more difficult, because I had a huge fear of being out of control. But he was patient, and with his help and the support of my friend and his guide, I was able to do it.

I've been channeling for others since 2006 in various ways. Sometimes I've done real-time trance channeling, allowing Shiva to innervate me and have a conversation with whomever I'm doing the channeling for. Other times, it's been via email, with me in full or partial trance while Shiva and I work together to type his responses. I also do relayed channeling, in which Shiva speaks to me and I pass along what he's saying. While trance channeling is the most effective, and it's most obvious to others that I'm actually channeling, some people find the energy shifts from Shiva's presence too intense, so relayed channeling is a good middle ground.

In my business practices, channeling has been an on-and-off thing. At times, I've lost confidence in my skills, and for several years the business as a whole was on hold so I could raise my kids. In 2019, I made the choice to stop having it be on-and-off, and go all in with offering channeling to my clients.

In 2020, I felt called to begin channeling short daily messages to post on social media. Being able to bring Shiva's words to a wide audience has been a joy-filled experience for me, especially as I've seen the messages make a difference for people. After a few months, I realized I was, unknown to me but quite likely with Shiva's full awareness, collecting material for a book as well as offering daily messages.

    This is that book. The messages contained here were originally posted on social media in August through December of 2020. Some of them were specific to the day or the time of year, so I asked Shiva to expand or revise them slightly. I've also reordered the messages by topic and theme rather than in the same order they originally appeared. Other than those changes and the correction of a few typos, the messages appear as they did when I first channeled them. This is intended to be the first volume of several, as I plan to compile the ongoing daily messages periodically to release them as well.

    It's my hope that you will find guidance and compassion through reading these messages, and perhaps create or restore your own connections with your guides—and with yourself.

    River Lightbearer
    Lynn, MA May 2021

*- Shiva's Introduction -*

## SHIVA'S INTRODUCTION

Greetings. I am called Shiva.

I am what some humans term a "being of light." This refers to beings who are not embodied, as are humans, and have never been so. Our energetic vibrations are high, which is not a judgment nor a point of superiority, but merely a statement of the fact that different beings, even amongst humans, have differing levels of energetic vibration. I am a being of pure energy, which some may see as light; on a more figurative note, I offer guidance for positive growth and development, or what some may term as "light work," though that is a human term and not one I use to describe myself.

For me, time and space are irrelevant; I see what you might call the "future" as clearly as, and often simultaneously with, what you consider to be the present. I am not the ultimate Creator, nor do I purport to speak for this consciousness. I speak merely from my own perspective as one who dwells closer to the Source than do humans, and who has existed for millennia and therefore has gained knowledge and experience beyond the scope of most humans.

## Shiva's Introduction

I choose to work with humans as a way of furthering my own growth, for there is no point at which any being can be said to have "finished" their growth and evolution. I do this work also because I enjoy interacting with humans, and those with whom I have chosen to act as a guide bring me great joy and humility, for I learn from them as much as they from me.

The messages in this book have been compiled by one of those humans, a person you may know as River Lightbearer or as Kim Ramsey-Winkler, and whom I have known through multiple of their lifetimes as Ganatram Shiva Das. This soul and I began our work together centuries ago, and through each of their incarnations, we have reconnected.

Ganatram asked me to collaborate with them to bring daily messages of guidance and compassion to the social media sphere, as it were, and I was happy to agree. This work is part of Ganatram's spiritual growth as well, and is, I hope, of benefit to those who read the messages.

We have chosen to compile the messages into this book, organized by theme and topic, for reference by any who feel they may benefit from the messages contained herein. It is my hope that you will read these messages and take from them what is relevant and beneficial to you.

I make no claims to be an authority. My wisdom is no greater than yours, merely different. If something you read in these pages does not resonate for you, heed your own intuition and wisdom over the words printed upon the page. One of the lessons I hope those who read this book will learn is that each of you is your own authority. Each of you is your own creative power, and each has the power and wisdom to discern truth from fiction, and wisdom from misleading information.

Read these words and take from them what you will. Know that as you progress through the messages, some will resonate and some will not. Some will cause you discomfort as they challenge deeply entrenched beliefs you have held for years; and often, this discomfort is an indication of a need to reexamine those beliefs and recognize a new truth.

Know that as you do this reading, this work, your own guides are with you. If you are unaware of them or have not yet forged a connection, know they are there nonetheless, and when it is time for you to recognize and connect with them, tools shall be presented to you to enable the safe accomplishment of this.

Each of you has guides; but beings and entities also exist who do not have your true benefit at heart. For this reason, I advise against endeavoring to connect with your guides without studying or being taught the safe means by which to do so. This information is something Ganatram and I shall release at a later date for those who wish to seek it; however, other resources are also available to you. Again, utilize your own discernment and guidance to locate the resources which will most benefit you in seeking this connection.

But connected or not, your guides are with you, and if you listen, they may guide you through your reading of my words in this book.

Trust what you read that feels true and right for you. Trust, too, any sense that what you are reading is not true or not to your highest ideal.

Read, discern, and know that you hold within you as much knowledge as this book holds within its pages.

You are infinite, beloveds, and you do know.

Be well and be loved.

Shiva
May 2021

## KNOW LOVE

From where does hatred come? From where does the belief that any human is lesser or does not deserve to exist come? Examine this within yourself if it is present. How does hatred and negation of others serve you? Where did you learn to think this way?

Love is the only constant throughout the Universe. Humans often reject one another, and in so doing reject love. And yet love permeates all of Creation. By rejecting it and choosing hatred, you reject Creation as a Whole.

Consider whether this is what you truly believe, and why you would wish harm and hatred upon any other. Toward whom do you truly direct these things?

Consider, and know you are loved regardless, perhaps even by those you choose to hate.

Throughout your life, you form connections to other humans. Sometimes these connections are negative and unpleasant. But many times, you form connections which are joyous and beneficial to you. At times, these positive connections are taken for granted.

Today, examine the connections in your life, both to people who are in your life at this time and to those who have departed. Focus upon the positive connections. Who in your life has helped you to feel love and joy? Whose presence in your life brought you benefit? In whose life has your presence brought love, joy, and benefit?

Take a moment today to honor those with whom you have experienced these positive connections. Even if they have departed your life, honor the memories you have of them. Be mindful as you consider these connections, and allow yourself to feel the joy they have brought you.

Love is not conditional. Not in its true form, coming from the Source and the Universe. Not in the form given to you by your guides and the other beings who wish humanity joy and growth.

Yet humans place conditions upon an emotion and call this emotion love. They claim to love their partners, their children, even all others...and yet place conditions upon that emotion. "I love you if you believe as I do." "I love you if you do as I say."

Learn to know love in its most genuine form. It is human nature to place conditions upon many things; however, it is imperative to learn to feel and accept love with no conditions. This is how your world and your people will truly heal. When love is accepted and expressed in its most genuine form.

You will learn, just as children learn to express themselves. You are children now, but growth will occur. Be patient.

Love is the most prevalent quality in the Universe, and yet it is one often abused by those who seek to use it for their own ends.

*- Know Love -*

When some of you speak of "light and love," you are speaking words which, while perhaps not intentionally false, are not true to what you mean. You do not exclusively feel love for others in the way you wish others to believe. "Light and love" can be a mantra one speaks to aspire to those qualities, but it is not a speech to give to paint yourself in a way others might see and admire.

Speak true words. If "light and love" is true for you, then by all means speak it. But if you know that inside your heart you feel negatively, you feel hatred and dislike, you feel anger and indifference, then be clear. If not to others, then at least to yourself.

Light and love are admirable. They are not the only qualities one must possess to live an authentic life. Be genuine about what you carry within you, and you will gain far more than if you merely speak empty words.

You are so deserving of love, and yet you reject love when it is offered to you. You reject it within yourself. Why is this so?

For those of you who have experienced harm at the hands--or words--of others, the answer is clear. You reject love because you have been taught or shown that you are unworthy of it. But that is false. Nothing about you has rendered you unworthy. That belief is only the remnants of others' harm.

Open your eyes and heart to the love around and within you. The love that you feel for others belongs to you as well. Allow yourself to receive it, both from others and from yourself.

You are abundantly worthy. Nothing any has said or done can change this.

Love is power. When you feel and experience love, it is a

powerful experience, but also brings power to you. It builds on the power you carry within you, and helps you see that power for what it is.

However, be mindful of seeking love from others as validation of yourself. When you are unable or unwilling to feel love for yourself, it is, despite what others say, entirely possible to feel love for others; but without feeling love for yourself you will be unable to *accept* love from others, and this disempowers you and them.

Love is the most prominent thing in the Universe. It is felt and experienced by all beings. Yet some of you reject it because you believe yourself unworthy or because others have harmed you in the name of "love," a false name in those cases.

Work to feel love for yourself. Even when it is difficult, even when it seems impossible, know that you are abundantly deserving of love, and that love needs come from you first and foremost. You are not alone in this effort. Those who do love you are with you and will aid you if asked.

How can you look upon yourself and see not beauty, but ugliness? How can you cast this ugliness upon others?

Yet this is what some humans choose to do. To see within themselves that which they hate and fear, and cast these things upon others as an excuse to hate and fear them as well. Some cannot embrace their true selves, and to cover up that which is too painful to face, they accuse others of possessing these qualities they themselves possess.

No one is deserving of hatred. Regardless of one's appearance, beliefs, or past, no one deserves to be held in a view which negates their very existence. For all those who carry even a spark of love and humanity, hatred destroys with no hope of new creation.

And yet some of you turn this hatred, this destruction, upon yourselves, and believe yourselves unworthy of love or

*- Know Love -*

redemptions. Beloveds, if you were truly beyond these things, you would not hold this belief, for love and redemption would be the furthest things from your minds. The fact that you fear yourself unworthy is a sign that you are, indeed, worthy and able to receive.

Your healing begins when you cease to view yourself as damaged beyond healing. Believe you can heal, and so it shall be.

How can you look upon yourself and not see the light and beauty within? For those who are outside of you, those things are so bright, so clear, that it seems impossible not to see.

Yet some of you struggle to see these things within yourself. Some of you have, in fact, been taught that those things do not exist within you, and therefore do not even think to look.

They are there. You carry light. You carry beauty. And you are wonderfully created.

Learn to look for and look at the light within you. What others have told you is false. You are beautiful.


Do you know how valuable you are? I speak not in terms of your value to others, but simply the value that is yours and is you by virtue of your existence.

Each action you take, each thought, each word, affects more than only you. Words you speak or write may reach people you will never know. The energy you put out may bring about profound change in other areas of the Universe. A single tiny action might ripple into massive change and growth.

Refrain from diminishing yourself. Resist the belief that you are insignificant or small. Each being, each consciousness, has a role to play in the Whole of the Universe.

You are one, but you are infinite. Know this to be true, and treat yourself as the incredible, valuable being you are. Allow love, both from within and from outside yourself.

For whom do you feel love? Many among you would name family, whether blood or chosen. Some would name friends or partners.

How many of you would name yourselves?

In the process of learning and engaging with the world around you as a small child, some of you have learned to love others at the cost of yourselves. Others of you have learned to love yourselves at the cost of others. Learn now to love yourself *and* others, and know there is no cost.

Love is an infinite. There are no limits. There is no "running out." Love exists everywhere, in and for all beings.

There is no need to exclude yourself from receiving it. There is no need to exclude others from it. You as an individual need not love all others, of course. Particularly when one has harmed you, you need not feel love for them, or indeed feel anything at all. But throughout the Universe, love is available for all.

Hatred is not the opposite of love. Hatred is negation and destruction. To hate is to deny the right to exist. Why would you choose to feel this for any being? How does it serve you?

How does it serve you to feel hatred for yourself? Do you not deserve to exist?

Examine within yourself the existence of love and hatred. Choose which you would prefer, and which would best serve you. And above all, learn, if you have not already, to feel love for yourself.

Among you are those who need this message more than others: You are loved. You are needed. You are valued. You, above all others, are unique in the Universe, and your presence brings light and joy. Your absence, though you

*- Know Love -*

believe otherwise, would be noted with sadness and pain.

You have fallen into a darkness of late, and this darkness convinces you that light does not exist anywhere, let alone within you. But I assure you that light is there.

Reach up out of the darkness. Seek the hands of those who will help you find the light once again.

You are loved. You are needed. You are wanted.

You are alive. We need you to remain so.

You are not alone.

*- Know Yourself -*

## KNOW YOURSELF

The first true step in the journey of your life is to know yourself.

This is a step at times overlooked or negated. You may be taught that you must choose your career path, your schooling, even your hobbies and social activities, based upon what others think. You are not taught to know who you are at your core, but who others want you to be.

In a healing journey, particularly, one needs to begin with knowing that core self. You cannot heal to become who you truly are if you are unaware of who you are at your core. That *is* who you truly are; how can you become this if you do not know what it is?

Spend time in connection with yourself. This may be through meditation, or simply sitting quietly. It may be through journaling, or reading books that call to you. It may be through communication with your guides or even through divination tools.

Whatever method works for you, I encourage and invite you to use it to gain a clearer understanding of your core self. This will benefit you greatly in your journey and in your work

*- Know Yourself -*

in the world.

Take time to listen to your core self.

What do you wish to achieve? What do you wish to gain? What do you wish to release?

Your life is yours to create as you will. You have the power to create whatever life you choose to live. You may do this on your own or with assistance, for you are not alone and how you choose to proceed is also up to you.

Look forward to the coming year as one in which you may create aspects of your life that better serve and benefit you, and know you have within you the power to make them real.

It is time to listen. To listen to the voice within you, the one that knows.

Each of you has a voice within. Some call it intuition, or conscience. Some call it guidance. Some call it nothing, for you deny it is there or assume it is your imagination.

Within you, each of you holds the key to creating the life you wish to live. Each of you holds the knowledge of what will truly benefit you--and of what must be removed for those benefits to manifest.

You seek guidance from others and attend to it yet ignore the guidance from within yourselves. Now is a time to cease ignoring what you know to be true. To cease denying that this voice within you has the knowledge you seek.

It is fine to seek answers from external sources, but listen first to the voice within.

Distractions abound in your world. Humans have created myriad ways to distract themselves from what pains them, what surrounds them, even from themselves.

Learn to release the need for these distractions. While

*- Know Yourself -*

they have their place and time, many of you have come to rely too heavily upon them, to the detriment of your growth and progress.

Learn to be with yourself without distractions. Learn to be in the world without relying upon other things to dull the pain and emotions.

Set down your phones, your computers, your televisions. Step away from these. Step outside and take time to be fully present in the place and time in which you find yourself. Resist the discomfort which steers you back toward your distractions.

Work to spend more and more time engaged fully in the moment, as you say. Distractions do not serve what you wish to bring to bear.

I invite you at this time to turn within.

This is a time for you to contemplate yourself. To sit in silence and solitude.

This prospect brings up fears within many of you. Even when you are quiet, you are often not truly silent. Even when you are by yourself, you are not truly alone.

However, learning your true self is the first step in the work you wish to accomplish in the world. You cannot see the world and your fellow humans for what and who they are until you have seen what and who you truly are.

Be unafraid of this task. Know that your guides are with you to support you as you learn.

Some of you will reject this task, and that is acceptable. In all things, you have choice. But for those who choose to accept, trust the truth and abundance you will reach through learning your true self.

Nothing which has occurred in your life has truly changed

*- Know Yourself -*

you. You have changed, yes, but those changes were not created by others or by events. Those changes come from within you.

When harm occurs, it does alter how you see the world. It alters how you see yourself. And these things cause it to appear that you yourself have been altered.

Within you is the core, the shining light around which your physical form was created. This core, this light, has not been dulled or damaged. This light still shines within you, and although you might not see it, it shines brightly for those who truly see.

Know that this light is there, and know that you carry it regardless of harm your past has caused you.

Seek this light within you, for that is the first step toward seeing it within others.

Know this light is there, and embrace it, for some of you fear it instead.

Know your true self, and healing shall occur.

Take time today to embrace all aspects of yourself. Each part of you has contributed to the whole of who you are, just as each of you has contributed to the Whole of the Universe.

Some aspects of yourself are no longer needed, and these may be released. However, refrain from rejecting or despising those aspects. Rather, acknowledge the contributions they have made in your life. The protection they have brought you, or the paths they have shown you.

Invite them to leave rather than pretending they do not exist. Inform them your need for their service has ended, rather than rejecting and denying their existence.

Treat these aspects as you would have wished yourself to be treated by others at the times in your life when those aspects were needed. And then allow them to go.

*- Know Yourself -*

You have grown. You have changed. But growth and change does not include denial of who you once were.

Darkness is nothing to be feared, yet many of you fear it, particularly when you realize it is within you.

This darkness, this "shadow self" as some term it, is not a monster or something which exists separately from you. It is part of who you are. By rejecting and seeking to eliminate it, you feed it. Fear and hatred feed that which you wish to remove.

Rather than seeking removal of this shadow, seek instead to embrace it. To nurture it, for the shadows and darkness within you are often formed from parts of your childhood self that were not nurtured or accepted. This is why rejection only feeds the negative aspects; these aspects have already been rejected a large number of times. They seek acceptance. They seek consolidation.

Embrace. Nurture. Accept these aspects as part of you and learn to work with them rather than against them. Even those that appear negative have gifts and protection to offer you should you choose to learn to recognize and accept it. Make this part of your healing work, for you cannot heal if you continue negating parts of yourself.

Listen carefully to the voice you hear within you. Not the voices of those from your past, nor even the voices of your guides, but the true voice of your core self.

Learning to hear this voice takes time, yet it is necessary if you are to grow and attain that which awaits you. You have learned to hide this voice even from yourself, as you have learned to hide your core self and the light it contains.

It is time now to learn otherwise; to learn to truly hear and to show your light. To show your truth. This is a time when what you carry and hide within you is needed in the world.

*- Know Yourself -*

Will you, then, continue to hide? Or will you risk coming out of hiding, risk heeding that voice, to bring about a time of beneficial events in your world?

Listen to that voice within you, for it will help you choose your course.

Step outside yourself for a moment. Observe yourself as if through the eyes of another. What do you see? Is it someone you truly wish to be, or are there things about the person you view that you might wish to change?

Many humans live lives in which they feel unhappy or unfulfilled. In which "busy" becomes the label for which they strive the hardest, as though it is an award to be won. Some even wallow in the life they live as if to seek accolades and praise for their "sacrifices."

This is not a statement of judgment upon any who live that way. There are at times uncontrollable circumstances which cause it. Even when circumstances are within one's control. They become entrenched in those lives.

But be aware of the reasons you remain in a life in which you do not experience joy. Even when not all aspects are within your control, over what *do* you have control? What change can you bring?

The praise of others means nothing when it comes at the cost of your own joy and happiness. Seek joy rather than praise. Seek the life you wish, rather than living a life which brings comments from others.

Often, gratitude is expressed toward others. For material possessions. Toward a higher power, should one be part of your beliefs.

When was the last time you chose to express gratitude toward yourself?

*- Know Yourself -*

Each thing you have in your life is there in part because you have created it. Your creative power has brought certain things into your life, and as you learn to harness that power, you shall bring in more benefits.

You are part of every interaction you have. You are part of everything that comes into your life.

Knowing this, knowing that you are as much to thank for what you have as is anyone else, use this day to show gratitude to yourself as well. Honor your own creative power as you honor others who have contributed positively to your life.

Remember who you are. At times, you forget this. You forget that you were created as a wonderful expression of Source. That you were created with power, strength, and grace. You forget that you carry light and beauty within you.

Remember who you are. Remember the power within you. Remember that you are worthy of love and abundance, and that when you recognize this, no one shall take these things from you.

Remember who you are. Honor yourself. Respect the person you are, have been, and will become. Know that you are where you need to be at this time, and that you are not the things you have done or experienced.

Remember who you are.

You have been told to "stop playing small." I tell you that you are not, and never have been, small. You are infinite, and yet miniscule at the same time. Each of you, each being, is a universe unto themselves even while being part of the glorious Whole of the Universe. And as that universe, you are not and cannot be "small," for any choice you make about how to present yourself is the right choice for you at that moment.

*- Know Yourself -*

Rather than seeking to be "big," seek to be *you*. Seek to show the world your true self, the self you may have hidden beneath layers of "should" and "have to" for all these years. It matters not at all whether you show this truth to one other or billions of others; each is valid, and each is immense. It matters only that you stop hiding, particularly from yourself.

Be you. As some humans are fond of saying, size does not matter. Simply be you.

Fear is understandable at this time, but know there are others waiting to embrace you when you are able to speak your truth despite the fear. You are not alone.


This is a time to draw within and tend to your needs, your emotions, your shadows. However, be mindful in so doing, for drawing within is not the same as withdrawing from the world.

Drawing within is focusing upon your own thoughts, emotions, needs, and desires. It is connecting to yourself and learning who you are at your true core. It is tending to the things you wish to change about yourself and addressing the aspects of yourself which cause difficulties.

However, in this process, the support and contact with others is more beneficial than ever. Denying yourself these things will lead only to further pain and struggles.

So as you focus inward for the work you would be wise to do, remember to keep the external connections that will aid you in this work.


In your quest to connect with something other than yourselves, to connect electronically, to be aware of all that occurs outside yourselves, you have lost touch with who you are.

Within you lies a true core. This is the "self" as whom you

*- Know Yourself -*

were created and birthed. This is the "you" underneath the pain, the harm, the experiences you have incurred throughout this life. At this core lies your true self and lies the healing and wisdom you often seek from external sources.

This is not to say that seeking outside yourselves is "wrong," for that is a judgement I do not make. Seeking truth and solace wherever you may find it is valid.

I encourage you, however, to seek these things within. To spend time in quietude and stillness connecting with your true core. It is there, although it may be hidden, and it waits for you to find it so that you may move closer to being whole and being part of the Whole.

When you doubt what you are capable of accomplishing, you limit your accomplishments.

When you doubt your capacity to heal and grow, you hinder that growth and healing.

Your limits are largely self-imposed, beloveds. While you are, by nature and necessity, limited in some ways by the physical forms in which you find yourselves, you are limited far less than you believe. Many of the limits you perceive to exist are there solely because you have decided it must be so.

Examine the limits you believe exist in your lives. Examine where those limits originated, and where the beliefs that caused them arose.

Part of the work you are invited to do consists of identifying and removing these limits from yourselves; for while you believe you are limited, you are unable to bring your gifts and skills fully into the world. And the world, the Universe, needs what you have to offer.

You are an infinite being.

I have said this previously, yet some of you doubt it. You

have identified yourselves with the forms in which you currently reside. You have identified yourselves with the limits of those forms.

Before you came to dwell within your current form, you were infinite. When your time of being within that form ends, as it must, you shall again become infinite.

The Universe itself is infinite, and each of you, each being of any type, is both a piece of and a reflection of the Universe. Therefore, how can you not be infinite in some way? You are created by and as Infinity itself.

These are concepts which may ring true to you, or not. They may feel uncomfortable for you, or not. Any response you have is valid.

Feel within yourself for the truth of your being, but only when you are ready to hear that truth, Whenever that may be, or if it does not come to pass at all, it—and you—are still valid and loved.

Be yourself. You hear these words frequently, with little context or meaning behind them. They have been spoken so often that they have ceased to have meaning.

I tell you that to be yourself, you first must know and accept who that is. And you must work past the fear that comes from allowing others to see your true self.

I speak now to those who do not fit the "boxes" your society has created. To those among you who seek relationships with people you were told are not the correct gender or shape or size. I speak now to those who seek connection with more than one.

I speak to those who do not fit the boxes of "male" or "female," or who are other than what they were told they were.

I speak to all of you who experience fear around what and

*- Know Yourself -*

who you are. To those who fear the reactions of others and harm from those others. To those who know you are something else and yet continue to attempt to be what you have been told you must be.

All of you have a place, and all have a right to be seen for who you truly are.

Step into the light and be seen. If doing so in the face of other people is unsafe for you, step out and allow the Universe to see that you recognize yourself and love yourself as you are loved.

## KNOW COMPASSION

    Today, step away from the overwhelming number of tasks on your list.

    Step away from the demands of others and that you have placed upon yourself.

    Step away from the perceived need to do things without end.

    Step, instead, into peace. Into stillness. Into nature if this is possible where you are.

    Step into breathing. Into the knowledge that your light cannot be contained and need not be restrained by lists and demands.

    Step into rest, for there is a need and a time for rest for all beings.

    Give yourself compassion at this time. No matter what you are struggling with, know that it is temporary; however, know also that it is acceptable to feel sadness or fear about the struggles.

You have learned to deny yourself the right to feel. It is time now to turn within and connect with your emotions. Creating abundance, creating positivity, necessitates a combination of reason and emotion. Denying or negating either one will lead to difficulties in building the life you wish to live.

Connect with yourself and know that emotions, whether positive or negative, are not the enemy. They are part of existence, and you are allowed to feel them.

How wonderful you are.

When you read those words, do you dispute them? In your mind, is a voice speaking contradictions and denials?

Beloveds, why do you doubt yourselves so? The Source from which you come created you to be beautifully, wonderfully made, and yet you believe yourself to be ugly and worthless.

Raise your heads. Look toward the sky. The sun and moon. Look around you at nature. Visit the sea or lake or river. Are these not wonderfully made?

They come from the same Source as you. If they are beautiful and wonderful, how can you be otherwise?

See yourself as you are, not as others and events in your life have led you to believe.

Refrain from making yourself responsible for all people and things within your life. You are not alone in all things. When you act as if you are the only one able or competent to complete certain tasks or accomplish certain things, you do a disservice to the others who are there to aid you, and to yourself as you place more pressure upon yourself than is needed.

*- Know Compassion -*

Examine the tasks in your life. Identify those which may be passed on to others, or which may be unnecessary at all.

You are one person, and although you are limitless within, limits such as time and physical capacity do exist. Be mindful of these.

Above all, remember that you are more important than the tasks on any list. You matter more than the things you do.

Be mindful of the words you speak. Each time you use hateful or harmful words toward yourself or another, you lower your vibration.

For some of you, the most frequent target of these damaging words is yourself. You wonder why your life continues to follow a negative path, and yet the words you speak in your confusion are part of the cause.

Each time you condemn yourself or berate yourself for not being where you believe you "should" be, you perpetuate the struggles. Each time you direct anger and hatred toward yourself, you mire yourself in the energy which creates the circumstance.

Be kind to yourself. Be kind to others. Speak words that raise vibration, that build peace and hope and healing. Speak words that honor you and your accomplishments, even when you have not accomplished what you wished.

Speak words that build you up rather than tearing yourself down, and watch your energy and circumstances change for the better. Know this to be true, and endeavor to create what you wish to create.

Your feelings are valid.

For some of you, that is a phrase you may not have heard before or have not heard enough in your life. You have been told you are "wrong" to feel as you feel, or that your feelings have no basis and are therefore invalid.

I tell you that if you feel, however you feel, it is true for you and therefore is valid.

Choose carefully how you respond or react to the feelings that arise within you, for it is in actions and words that pain and harm may lie, or that choices may be made that are unwise or damaging. Actions and words can be unwise.

But emotions are part of being human, and they are valid. You are valid. Allow yourself to feel as you feel and reject statements by others that your feelings are not allowed or are not "right."

Healing is not a linear path, and yet some of you treat it as such. You condemn or reject those who are not constantly making forward progress in their journeys--even when that person is you yourself.

All journeys have twists and turns. Healing particularly, for as you heal one part of yourself, other parts which need healing will become evident. Other issues which hold you back or cause you pain will come to the fore.

Accept that healing is a journey which will occupy the remainder of your life, and accept and honor that at times, this journey may appear to have stopped or even reversed. Accept this and show compassion to those—including yourself—who have chosen to undertake a healing journey, for this is not a journey for the faint of heart. Healing takes courage. Refrain from underestimating this.

Some of you have been taught that seeking help is shameful. That you must do for yourselves, and that you are solely responsible whether you succeed or fail. You have been taught that illness is weakness, and that need is undesirable.

None of these things are truth. They are fictions passed

*- Know Compassion -*

along from generation to generation by those who were too fearful or stubborn to understand that no one need struggle alone.

Reaching out for help is no cause for shame. It is strength, for asking for help requires the strength to trust. Illness is not weakness; it is merely a limitation of your physical form. Failure is an illusion; there is no failure, there is only growth and learning, although you may grow and learn things you did not foresee or desire.

Learn to release the fear and shame of seeking help when it is needed. Learn to show the strength to say, "I need help."

This is a way of connecting, and as you are helped, so shall you help others in time.

When you are tending to a task and are distracted by external factors, it is human nature to become annoyed or frustrated. However, while feeling these emotions is acceptable and understandable, allowing yourself to indulge or wallow in the frustration or annoyance does not change the situation.

Work to change how you respond to the external factors which distract or disrupt your tasks and routines. These are not being done maliciously or to cause you difficulty. Life often interferes or intervenes in what you wish to do. Learning to embrace and use your creative power includes learning to control and choose, mindfully, your responses when something unpleasant occurs.

Breathe, release the thoughts which arise from the negative emotions, and resume your task, or, if unable to resume, find another task which soothes and calms you.

It is acceptable to feel as you feel. Your responses to those emotions are what can make a difference in your life.

*- Know Compassion-*

Some of you push yourselves to the breaking point day after day. You feel that you must complete and accomplish thing after thing, with no regard for yourself or your health or limits.

Beloved, allow yourself time to rest. You are not measured by what you do. Your worth does not depend upon how much you accomplish.

Allow yourself to rest. To breathe. To be.

Sometimes the busy-ness is used to mask thoughts and emotions with which you do not wish to deal. You push yourself to avoid sitting with your thoughts. While this is understandable, your thoughts also deserve room to breathe. If they are difficult for you to manage or are frightening to you, seek support in being with them, but refrain from causing yourself exhaustion and illness to avoid those thoughts.

Allow yourself to rest. To breathe. To be. And know that you have love and support.

Breathe.

At times you place too much pressure upon yourself. You become immersed in the stresses and strains of daily life, and you forget the most important, most fundamental task.

Breathe.

I say this literally as well as figuratively, for the very act of breathing can soothe you. It connects you to the world around you. It brings you "out of your head," as it were, and into a deeper fullness of understanding and peace.

Breathe.

At times, your mind races so quickly it is immeasurable. Thoughts and emotions swirl around as snowflakes within a blizzard. This leads to anxiety, to fear, to overwhelm, and at times you collapse under the weight of the speed at which

*- Know Compassion-*

your mind runs.

    Beloveds, you have the power to slow yourselves. You have the power to end the swirling and spirals. Even when it feels as if your minds and thoughts are beyond your control, they are not. You are simply unable to recognize this.

    This does not mean you are choosing to have these anxieties and fears. This is not a conscious action on your part, and therefore is not by your choice. However, it is our hope that you may learn to recognize that you have the choice to bring the swirling and spirals to an end when they occur.

    Begin with a breath. One slow, deep breath. Feel the floor or ground beneath you. Feel the chair upon which you sit, or the air as it circulates around you.

    These tools shall aid you in gaining and using the power you have to slow your mind and soothe yourselves.

    At this time, so many of you are feeling overwhelmed by all that is occurring in your world. Take time to rest, beloveds.

    You see the road you need travel, and yet are blind to how far you have already come. Does not the completion of even part of your journey warrant a time of rest and recuperation?

    You serve no one when you push yourself beyond your breaking point, so to speak. You serve no one when you allow yourself to become so overwhelmed you cannot think straight.

    Step back. Sit. Breathe.

    Know, as you already know deep within yourself, that all shall be well, and that it is acceptable to stop and rest for a time.

    Be gentle with yourself at this time. You have experienced pain and fear over the past months. Your world has entered a state of near-constant darkness, both as a whole and within the minds of some of those who claim to lead you. This

*- Know Compassion-*

darkness has now begun to abate, and yet it shall linger a while longer, as humankind learns to seek and live in light once again.

Be patient with yourself and others as the harm which has been done begins now to unravel and be replaced with light. Learn compassion for yourself as you struggle with the aftereffects of things that have occurred in your individual life and in the life of your world as a whole.

Allow yourself to rest over the coming weeks, for it is a time for rest and recovery. Know that things shall begin now to change, and in time, you will be part of that change. But for this moment, show yourself the respect of allowing rest.

Among you there are those who become angry or fearful when things do not go as planned. This is an effect of your pasts, but also of your expectations. You are not expected to complete everything. You need not take on the responsibilities for everything in the world.

Yet you believe yourselves responsible for so much that is outside of your responsibility, and you condemn yourselves when your plans do not reach fruition or when you are unable to rise to the impossible tasks you have set before yourselves.

Beloveds, show yourselves compassion. Your measure is not the number of things you accomplish or the accolades and certifications you achieve. You are abundantly worthy of love solely by virtue of your existence.

Let your measure be the good you place into the world rather than numbers and pieces of paper. For you yourselves are your own measure.

So many of you feel overwhelmed by all that is occurring in your world at this time. You wish to change things. To heal them. To make things go away, as it were.

*- Know Compassion-*

You are reaching out into a broad world with many things occurring, and yet question why you feel overwhelmed, why you are experiencing stress, anxiety, depression, and other negatives.

You are seeing too broadly at times. So for today, look more closely around you. Turn your focus to what is outside your window, within view of your physical eyes. To what is within your home and heart.

You wish to change the world, but for today, narrow your view to focus upon what you have around you. Both the joyous things which you may take for granted and the less pleasant things over which you have control. It is not selfish to take joy in what you have, nor is it selfish to focus upon yourself, your health, and your life for a time.

Allow yourself to breathe. In the stress and strain of daily life, this is a simple thing you sometimes forget to do or of which you become unaware.

Take a moment today to experience each breath. To marvel at the body's ability to fuel itself with something as invisible and intangible as air. Feel each breath enter your body and expand throughout. Connect to the breaths you take, and through them, to the air, the earth, the water. The power.

Humans take many things in their lives for granted. Today, choose not to let breathing be one of those things.

Close your eyes. Breathe deeply. Feel yourself whole and full.

Know that this peace is here for you at any time. Many of you eschew it, for sitting in stillness is foreign and uncomfortable to you.

Some of you are adept at it and yet your egos tell you that

*- Know Compassion -*

you are better than those who are not adept.

Some of you have found the balance and know that this peace is here for you whenever you choose.

I speak to those who are afraid of stillness or whose egos believe they are "better at it."

This is a gift available to any who choose it, and there is no right or wrong way to achieve or receive it. It is here for you. Simply close your eyes and breathe.

You have no need to prove yourself to others.

At times, you push yourself beyond your capabilities in order to demonstrate to someone else that you are capable, that you are competent, that you are somehow worthy.

This is unnecessary, and it is harmful to you. You have no need to prove to any that you are worthy, for "worth" is an illusion. You are wonderful and deserving as you are created. There is nothing to prove.

Be gentle with yourself and be mindful of behaving in a way intended to prove anything to another, for doing so does not benefit you.

Take time to be with yourself. To contemplate yourself as an infinite being, and as a human who is bound by the limitations of that existence. To contemplate and comprehend the beliefs you hold and discern whether they are truly yours, or a default you have chosen because you were told to by others.

Take time to be. Not to think or do, but to be and to listen to what lies within you. Take time to love and to open to the potential for growth and understanding.

Take time.

Take time.

*- Know Compassion-*

Often, it is human nature to move quickly from one task to the next. Your life is built on and measured by that which you accomplish, and the more you accomplish, the higher your measure--or so you believe.

Take time in your tasks. Be fully present as you complete each of them. You need not rush from one to another. The quantity of tasks you complete is not the measure of who you are.

Take time to feel your emotions about the tasks. Take time to put your full attention and capacity into them. Take time to bring quality to them rather than seeking to prove that you can accomplish many things.

Take time.


Gratitude is a concept sometimes misused or misunderstood by humans.

When one expresses gratitude, it is felt and appreciated. But one need not express gratitude for what has caused harm or pain.

At times, it is said that one should "thank" the negative experiences in their life, and even "thank" their abusers, for providing life lessons. And for some of you, that is impossible. You cannot feel gratitude for being harmed or damaged.

This is acceptable. You need not feel or express gratitude for that which has harmed you. You need not seek to find "lessons" in damage that has been done to you.

Gratitude is something you may choose, or not. It is something which is entirely individual to each of you. None may tell you that you "must" feel gratitude. It is a choice you have available to make.

Choose what feels most helpful and healing to you, and release the "musts" and "shoulds."

*- Know Compassion-*

Seasons change. This is taken as a fact when one speaks of the turn of seasons within the natural world, but it is forgotten or brushed aside when one speaks of one's life.

Your life goes through seasons just as does the world. These seasons may look different and may not match with what is happening outside your windows, but they are vital to life nonetheless. Allow the seasons you experience. Accept what occurs within them. Know that even when you are in a season in which you appear to lie fallow or become stagnant, these too are times of growth and change.

Allow yourself to be in whatever season your life holds at this time. Know that it will bring you closer to the life you wish to create.


You are limitless, and yet you have limits. This contradiction, this dichotomy, causes you struggles. You do not understand how it is you can be both limitless and limited.

Your souls, beloveds, have no limits. Your hearts. Your desire for change and healing. These things are limitless, as is the abundance and support in your life from powers both seen and unseen.

Your physical forms, however, are limited. You have limits upon the physical and mental activities of which you are capable. Your bodies require rest and sleep, food and air. Some of you live with illness that causes further limits.

It is important to learn the difference between the limits you artificially place upon yourself out of fear or "don't-wanting," as one might say, and the limits which truly exist and of which you must be mindful in order to complete your work in the world.

Honor those true limits. Release your shame at not being able to accomplish as much as you would like, at needing to rest, at needing assistance.

Know your limits, but know too that at your core, you are

*- Know Compassion-*

indeed limitless.

## KNOW TRUST

Your world is in chaos at this time. So many changes have occurred. So many people are fighting and in conflict over right and wrong. There are those who claim conspiracies from everyone including those of us from beyond your world. There are those who claim none of this exists.

Know your place in the world. At this time. It is more vital than ever that you who are called to serve and aid others come to the fore. Be mindful of overextending yourself; your health, safety, and stability are important. However, reach out to those who are struggling and learning. Some will grow in negative directions, but many will come to the side of help and healing. You will be one to guide them there.

Know the truth. Not what others tell you is true, but what you feel deeply inside. There are no conspiracies. There is no "hoax." This is real, and it is time for you to step into reality and work to improve it.

This world has become a divided and divisive place. A

place where darkness seems to encroach ever further upon the lives you strive to live. Where it feels as if, at times, hope is lost.

It is not. Although I do not speak of absolute futures, I wish to assure you at this time that hope still exists, and that in time, the darkness and neglect shall change. Your lives shall reach a place of safety.

All struggles shall not end, for this is not the way of life. However, the immediate circumstances which cause your fear and despair are already beginning to shift.

Hold onto your hope, beloveds. Hold onto the trust that all shall be well. I am with you, as are many beyond your world. We shall hope with you and hold you in our hearts as your people reach a place and time of change.

Trust. I can tell you nothing more important than this. Trust and hope.

Many of you have experienced struggles and hardships over the past months. While you may hope for a more positive year to come, your fears are impacting what you wish to bring into your lives.

This is not to say that you "should" not feel fear. All emotions are valid, and all deserve to be felt and acknowledged. However, your thoughts, which are more within your control, may impact your ability to see positive opportunities and outlets.

Know that, while difficulties may remain for a time longer, your world is shifting to a more beneficial time. That which has held you back over the past months is coming to an end, and the way shall be opened to higher benefit. You need only be patient and trust that all shall be well.

Know that you are not alone and know that benefit will come.

*- Know Trust -*

Many of you seek reassurance from outside yourselves that all shall be well. You seek to hear from others, both seen and unseen, that the world will repair and restore itself, that things will return to "normal," that there is light and love.

Why do you seek this reassurance from external sources, when the answers and truth lie within each of you? This is a time when too many have turned to external sources for wisdom and truth, and as a result seize hold of untruth and darkness and have rejected their own knowing.

Asking for answers outside yourself is acceptable, but learn to seek truth first within yourself. You know, beloveds. You know the answers. You know how to make things well in your world.

When another gives you information that you feel deeply to be untrue or unwise, why do you choose to heed it despite that inner voice? Why do you choose to heed others over yourself?

Learn to believe and trust what you know within yourself to be true, for this is a way in which your world will grow. When each learns to believe what they truly feel rather than believing an "expert" solely because they have designated themselves such, the world will begin to heal.

The clarity you seek does not lie within others, but within yourselves. You know more than you recognize. You comprehend more than you believe.

Others may answer your questions and clarify your situations, but they can do so only from their own perspectives. Their ways of seeing and perceiving may not be yours and may not be true for you even if they are true for them.

Reach out for support, for solace, for answers as you desire, but reach within also. Trust yourselves above what others may tell you if what others say feels untrue or does not resonate for you.

No "expert" knows you better than you know yourselves. Bear this in mind as you seek.

You are abundantly capable of determining the most beneficial course for your life, and yet you hesitate out of fear of deciding incorrectly.

I encourage you to look for your answers within yourself, and to trust that you are correct.

If you choose "wrongly," and I use that term as it is often spoken although it is not a true concept, you may change your course. There is no action you may take as you choose the course of your life that cannot be either undone or altered.

Release the fear of being "wrong," and instead embrace the abundant possibilities which lie before you. Choose what you wish to choose and know you may change if the choice does not work as you hope.

Listen to the voice within you. This is a reminder to you that you know. You feel truth, and your feeling is valid.

What is true for you may not be true for another; what is true for them may not be true for you.

I encourage you to determine your own truth. If this matches what another says, so be it. If not, that, too, is what is.

Strive to accept your knowledge of truth above what someone else proclaims as such if their proclamation does not resonate for you.

Be mindful of those who loudly proclaim what they call truth, for at times the loudest proclamations are the ones most deliberately false.

Listen to your own inner voice and know that it speaks your truth.

Refrain from attempting to push things to occur faster than they are. Impatience is not a bad quality, for at times being impatient to make positive changes can lead to the recognition of new ways to create or change your life. However, impatience when directed toward others, or when it leads to anger and frustration that things are not occurring as fast as you would like, is not of benefit.

Know that all things happen in their own time. This is a precept which is taught in some of your religions and other paths. For all things, there is a time. And this time may not be what you wish it to be.

But know also that, while you cannot control the time in which things occur, you can control how you respond to the amount of time things require. You may choose to accept that something will take longer than you would prefer. You may choose to examine and acknowledge your emotions without becoming mired in them.

What you desire to occur shall happen when it is time for it to do so. As you wait, stay the course and know that things shall improve.

The thought of connecting and engaging with your guides and the other beings who seek connection and communion with humans frightens some of you.

This is understandable. We are not cause for fear, but there are others who do wish harm and malevolence.

However, you fear to the exclusion of all. You fear to the point that you hear your guides speaking to you and recognize them as benevolent, yet reject what they say because you question, or because you believe it cannot be real.

Those who wish to support and guide you will bring you no harm, and you will learn to trust your instincts as to who the benevolent ones are.

*- Know Trust -*

Trust your own instincts, however; for some of those humans who claim communion with positive beings have been misled and deluded.

It is a difficult journey. Learning to trust and recognize us is not easy. However, know that your guides are with you, ready to connect when you are ready to trust the connection.

Many beings speak to you at this time with words of comfort and succor. While I, too, offer you comfort and assure you that all shall be well, I and others wish to remind you also that you have power. You are able to make alterations in your world.

Now is not a time to simply "sit back and trust." Trust is necessary, indeed, but so is action. So is belief in your own innate power to create a life you wish to live.

Trust and know that all shall be well, but as you trust, work to make things well.

At this time, listen to the call within yourself. You are being drawn to something which will bring hope or healing to yourself and others, yet you reject this call. You question whether it is true or imagination. You doubt your capabilities.

Listen to what your intuition and inner power call you to do. Were you incapable, you would not be hearing this call. Trust in your power and ability to bring healing, to raise hopes.

Today, listen, and follow what you hear.

Be receptive. Listen to the wisdom that comes to you, both from within and from without. Learn to recognize when you are hearing true wisdom versus when you hear that which you wish to hear, or when you hear false statements or beliefs that do not work for you. But listen, nonetheless.

*- Know Trust -*

Too many of you reject what you hear as "imagination" or as something which would not work, even though you have no experience of it. Too many of you have learned to "tune out," as it were, the wisdom and guidance given to you by others both seen and unseen.

Learn to open once again to the wisdom around and within you.

Many things in your life are not as they appear at this time. Your sight and understanding of these things are obscured by what you expect to see, so you are unable to see what is truly there.

Open your eyes, beloveds. Remove the blinders of expectation and anticipation and allow yourself to truly see what is there for you.

Some of what appears may not be to your liking, and yet this is the way of things. What arrives in your life will not always be what you wish to have or achieve. Living does not mean having all that you desire, but also means learning to desire what you have.

Open your eyes, for you are missing wonders and joy by refusing to see what is in front of you in favor of regretting what you do not have.

Open your eyes and see that your life will be better for having done so.

In your world, there are those who seek to harm or damage others. It is a sad fact of human life that this is so.

However, when you have been harmed, often you see harm where none exists. You project upon others the fears and damage which have been caused to you and assume malevolent intentions where there are no such intentions.

Awaken from that fear. Part of your work in healing from

*- Know Trust -*

harm and trauma is to learn to recognize when ill intent truly exists, and when it is your own mind and fear playing tricks upon you.

When there truly is harm or malevolent intent, take steps to protect yourself. But first discern objectively whether this malevolence is real or is the effect of what has gone before in your life.

Work to assume positive intent until shown otherwise from those who have not been involved in causing you harm. Work to assume positive intent on your own part in the actions and words you choose.

This is part of healing. And you are not alone in this work.

Today, you are called to be receptive. Be open to receiving from others that which you do not contain within yourself, as well as that which you do.

Be open to receiving love and compassion.

Be open to receiving information and wisdom.

Be open to receiving knowledge.

Be open to receiving that which you may wish to reject or are reluctant to accept, for within these things there is benefit for you. You resist or feel reluctance due to fear and your ego endeavoring to keep you in one spot.

Life is growth, and to grow, one must at times receive.

Why do you question your own heart? Some of you have come to believe ill of yourselves. To question whether you truly love or merely wish to gain from others. You have become swayed by those who have stated you are not a good person, or who question your motives.

You know yourself to be one with heart. One who feels love as it is intended. Yet you doubt yourself to the extent that you come to believe others know you better than you know yourself.

Release their words. You are the only one who truly knows your heart. The people who speak poorly of you, who call your motivations into question, who state that you act out of malice, are simply reflecting what is within them, and projecting it upon you.

If you are living your life in ways that harm none, and endeavor to bring love and healing, then you have no cause for concern. However, if you know that you are acting at times out of a desire to gain, or out of ulterior motives, examine why you do this. Make these decisions, these examinations, from what you know to be true, not because others have made accusations against you. True change comes only when you make it due to seeing the need, not when you make it to impress or persuade others.

Know your heart and believe your own perception of who you are.

Why do you refuse to trust yourself? Actions others have committed against you are no flaw or fault of yours. Unwise choices you have made in your life and likewise not fault or flaw. They are simply things which have occurred.

"But I have harmed others," you say, and that may be so. However, if you are aware of what you have caused and feel remorse for doing so, why do you not trust yourself to avoid those actions in the future?

Trust is the foundation upon which love and power are built. While love and power are entwined, without trust, the rest falls into the sea, as it were.

Examine the areas in which you distrust yourself. Why has this distrust developed? How can you change it?

Know that your guides are with you on this journey and will assist you if asked. Call upon them and upon others for whom you do feel trust to help you regain and build the trust in yourself.

Refrain from allowing yourself to be swayed by the words of others. Sometimes those who are the most incorrect or harmful in their words are those who speak the loudest.

Learn to discern truth and love for yourself rather than relying upon others to do so for you. Learn to recognize and understand your own beliefs, what you stand for, rather than forming your beliefs and opinions based upon who speaks the most forcefully.

You know the truth within yourself. Hear it and heed it. Stand up for what you believe even if it goes against the tide, as it were.

Many of you have been taught that you know little. That you must attend to and trust the words of those who call themselves experts above what you know to be true.

This is not the case. Training can make one an expert in that area, but even experts do not know everything. While it is important to listen to those who have learned and gained knowledge, it can be equally important to listen to the voice within yourself that identifies truth from falsehoods and inaccuracies.

This is not to say you should ignore the words of experts. You should heed the words of those who know and who speak facts. However, you should also heed the knowledge within yourself of whether what they say is true and beneficial.

Harm none is the first precept upon which one might build their life and beliefs. We urge you to live your life by this. Harm none and recognize harm where it exists.

Seek answers from others, but seek also within yourself. Trust the knowledge you feel and hear within you, for you are

*- Know Trust -*

connected to a larger Whole, and you know more than that for which you give yourself credit.

Others have knowledge and wisdom to impart to you, and there are certainly times when it benefits you to heed this. However, discern for yourself what is true and factual, and what is merely a matter of opinion and beliefs.

Facts are true. They are set. While knowledge may be gained over time which changes the facts that are presented, they are provable and can therefore be believed.

But not all is factual. Learn to recognize the difference between facts that can be proven and opinions which cannot. Learn to recognize truth from falsehoods or from that which is subject to interpretation and perception. Learn to believe yourself and believe in yourself, for you are wise and infinite, though that wisdom and infiniteness may be obscured by the form and circumstances in which you find yourself.

Celebrate yourself as part of the Whole of Creation, and celebrate your wisdom and knowledge.

Throughout your lives, humans are taught that they must abide by what others tell them. You must cleave to the beliefs and teachings of your parents, your schools, your places of worship. You must believe and live by the information dispensed to you by experts--even when those people are not truly experts but merely have declared themselves to be.

It is time for you to learn now that thinking only what you are told to think does not serve you. It does not benefit you as an individual or your world as a whole.

Take time to search within yourself for what you know to be true. Do not reject facts or science; those are things which exist and which are true. Your kind, humankind, has been given this knowledge for a purpose, and it is real and accurate. But question opinions and beliefs. Question that which cannot be proven. Come to your own conclusions rather than the

*- Know Trust -*

conclusions you are told must be yours.
    Within you, you hold vast knowledge and understanding. It is time to access it.

    Look within for the answers you seek. Many of you seek answers and wisdom from outside yourselves. While this can be of benefit to you, the most beneficial wisdom dwells within you.
    As you seek, remember to seek what lies within your mind, soul, and heart. Be mindful of excluding this for the sake of what others tell you.
    You contain more knowledge than that of which you have awareness. Learn to connect with what lies within.

## KNOW POWER

Power comes from within. It is not something one holds over another, though this is a definition often given. Power over another is not true strength; it is weakness, for it is dependent upon the other allowing that power to exist. This is not to say that one who is subjugated by another is choosing to be so; but if that one who is subjugated chose to rise up, the other would lose their power.

Only those who are weak of mind and spirit seek power *over* others. The truly strong, the truly knowing, seek power within themselves, knowing that that is true power.

Seek your inner power. Use it to create the life and changes you wish to see. And know this is strength.

Your life is your own. Your heart, mind, and soul are your own.

Why, then, do some of you choose to allow others power over your life? Over your heart and soul?

For some of you, that power has been taken forcefully, and I encourage you now to seek help in breaking that hold another has upon you. This is not by your choice, nor is it something you "allow," but you have the power to seek aid in stopping it.

For others who have willingly given over their power, I encourage you now to reclaim it. Know that you alone are the proprietor of your life, and you alone have the right to choose what sort of life you create. If you have chosen to allow another this power, now is a time to stop that allowance.

Those who seek to silence you about your experiences and emotions are those who struggle with their own.

None has the right to prevent you from speaking your truth, whatever that truth may be. When another strives to silence you or coerces you into speaking only in a certain way or thinking only certain thoughts, this is incorrect action on their part and is an attempt by them to control that which they struggle to control within themselves.

Negative emotions do not prevent the creation of positive events and occurrences. Light and darkness, positivity and negativity, these things must coexist for the Universe to remain in balance—and for each individual to maintain balance in their own lives and creations.

Allow yourselves to speak. Do so in gentle, nonharmful ways, but allow it nonetheless, for through speaking truth comes healing.

For some of you, the concept of having power in your life, and having the power to change the world, is frightening. It need not be so. You are not obligated to use your power for anything. You may choose simply to say you are powerless, and this choice is valid, though the statement is untrue. However, if you believe it to be true, so it is, while remaining equally false.

For some of you, power itself is frightening. You have seen others misuse and abuse their power in ways that have harmed you and others. Know that power used to harm is not true power.

True power lies within each of you. Each of us, for it exists in all beings, not only humans. This is the power to change. To create. To bring darkness out of the shadows and shed light upon it, for though darkness and light do and must coexist, bringing darkness into the light allows change to occur.

Release the fear of your own power. Learn to embrace that power. Learn to create your life and world as you truly wish to live it.

Your home is a place which you might consider a sanctuary, and yet some of you allow negativity and toxicity to enter your domain.

This is a choice you make. You allow people into your homes whom you know carry negative energy and have no benevolent intentions, yet they enter your home at your invitation because you believe you have no choice.

Just as you choose who enters your life, you choose who enters your home. And no degree of connection or relationships gives anyone free passage.

If someone is causing you pain, harm, or even discomfort, you may exclude them from your home. You are not obligated to allow them in.

Allow your home to be the sanctuary, the safe place, you need for your healing. Deny entry to those who interfere with that safety and security. You have that power.

There are those among you who question whether you have the "right," for want of better terms, to remove people from your life when they have wronged you or caused you harm.

I assure you, your life is your own. When another has

become toxic to you, or persists in knowingly causing you pain or damage, they have no right to remain within your sphere.

Your life is your own, and who is or is not part of that life is solely your choice.

I hear you now. "But they are family. But he is my husband. But she is my partner." Do you truly wish to allow these roles to be held by someone who would intentionally cause you pain?

Your health, both physical and mental, matters more than ties of blood or legality. You may, of course, choose to allow these people to remain, but there is no requirement to do so. Do you not deserve a life free of toxins and hate?

Make the wisest choice in your highest ideal. And, for those who need these words, remember that family is not blood, not legalities; it is those who love and accept one another without condition. And it can be chosen.


Refrain from debates and arguments with those who see the world differently from you. You will not convince them of your views, nor will they convince you of theirs.

In this time, your world has become divided among many points of view and beliefs. Some even question facts or dismiss them as opinions, yet they are rejecting things which have been proven beyond doubt.

Even those people will not be swayed, however. To endeavor to change them, to change their views, to persuade them of truth whether factual or not, will only cause harm to both of you.

Your first responsibility is to care for yourself. Placing strain upon yourself by indulging in conflict to no end does not serve you.

Speak the truth as you know it, particularly when such truth is undeniably proven. But do so without engaging with

*- Know Power -*

those who would refute you. This is power: the power to speak truth without causing pain or stress. The power to tend to your own knowledge and beliefs without the need to convince others of them. Claim this power.

How is it that some of you believe you have the right to tell others what is in their hearts? It is not for you to state others' thoughts or feelings.

Some of you do this in an effort to help, not realizing that it can, in fact, hinder the growth of those others. This is a case where you are well-meaning but are not causing the results you hope.

Sadly, some attempt to tell others what they are thinking or feeling in an effort to gain control over those others. To blame others for things of which they are not the cause, or for which the person making the claim has equal responsibility.

Some so-called leaders will fall to this tactic in order to attract followers and maintain their following, to build their empire, as it were, by tearing down others.

Be mindful of those who state others' minds and hearts. Of those who say things such as "You do not truly wish to heal, even though you say you do," or "Your intention was this, although you say it was that." Be mindful of following those who gain power by disempowering those around them.

Be mindful of becoming one of these people yourself. Seek understanding of others rather than power over them. Seek power only within yourself.

We speak often of "the world," as if all beings and entities and souls are one amorphous form. Although all of you are part of one glorious Whole, still each of you is also individual and separate.

Many of you seek change in "the world" and rail against

*- Know Power -*

things in "the world" with which you do not agree, yet you are unable to see your place and role within this "world" of which you speak.

Before seeking and demanding grand change throughout "the world," look first to the changes you might make within yourself.

Each bit of change, of learning, of growth, impacts the Whole. Each thing you consider and change within yourself brings change to your world.

Start small, beloveds. Start with yourself. Yes, you wish to—and shall—bring about change to the world, but only when you are willing and able to confront yourself and bring about the small changes first. You have the power to create the life you wish to live in the world in which you wish to live it. Embrace this power and use it wisely.

When you seek to bring about change, first seek within. What might you change about yourself that will facilitate the broader changes you wish to make in your world?

Remember that all is interconnected. Even when you believe you are not a contributor to the issues you seek to resolve, something within you may be changed that will aid in that resolution.

Look within. Your power lies within yourself, not over others or over the actions others commit. Seek first to change what truly lies within your power, and trust that these seemingly small changes will ripple outward to assist in the broader changes you wish.

Love surrounds you, yet some of you reject it. You find yourselves unworthy of love. You judge yourselves harshly, and sadly, this judgment extends to others.

Before you can truly embrace life and the others who live

*- Know Power -*

alongside you, you must clear away the self-hatred. Learning to see clearly who you are and what dwells within you is no easy task. For some, it will take years. For some, it is a journey upon which you will be for the remainder of your life.

However, I urge you to take the first steps of this journey. To seek healing within yourself. Some who call themselves healers are, in truth, deeply wounded inside, and are not tending to their own wounds before attempting to tend to others.

Be one who tends to your own wounds first. Seek the help you need to heal the damage within. No one is irreparably damaged. Within each of you dwells the perfect being as which you were created. One need not be "fully healed" to work to heal others; this is, in fact, nearly impossible. But one must be tending to one's own wounds before endeavoring to tend to others.

You have the power to heal. Exercise this power first upon yourself.

Each of you has free will. This is the most important gift you were given upon your creation. You have the power to choose your path, to choose your actions and words, to choose the life you wish to create.

However, in exercising this gift, you must remember that others also have the same gift. Your free will does not extend to depriving others of theirs. Your free will shall not impinge upon others' right to safety and to their lives.

Free will comes with the responsibility to ensure that your choices are beneficial. When you choose ways that cause harm, this is your responsibility. Too many claim that it is up to others to not be hurt, when the reality is you are granted the gift of freedom with the understanding that you will first cause no harm.

Seek to cause no harm. Casting blame upon others or

*- Know Power -*

saying they are unevolved or unenlightened when they suffer harm at your hands is a sign that you need further growth. Accept the responsibility that comes with this gift, for accepting your own responsibility for the actions and words you choose is the most necessary step in growth and awakening. You have the power to choose to take this step.

Peace is something for which many of you strive, and yet you continue a cycle of negative creations. You claim to desire peace, and yet perpetuate conflict and, as you might say, drama. You speak to others of the pain they cause, and do not recognize that you are doing the same to them as that of which you accuse them.

Peace. It is a fleeting thing, intangible, yet achievable when you look toward your own contributions to the contrary. It is not for others to change in order to create the peace you desire. This is something you must do for yourself.

Of course peace becomes wider-ranging and longer-lasting the more people contribute to it, but refrain from seeking to change others in order to achieve what you call peace. Instead look within at what you might change about yourself. You are the ultimate creator of your life. Know that you have this power and learn to utilize it.

## KNOW RESPONSIBILITY

Responsibility is the root of power. When you are unwilling to take responsibility for your choices and actions, how can you access the power that lies within you to create a positive life for yourself? How can you access the power within you to make this world better?

All things you do are choice. Humans often fall back on phrases such as "I have to" or "I have no choice," but in truth, there is always a choice. The other alternatives might be ones you dislike, or even ones which would cause harm; but still, they are there. They exist. Choice exists.

When you recognize where choice exists, you recognize the responsibility you have to make the most beneficial choice, and you accept the responsibility for the choices you make. And in recognizing and accepting this responsibility, you are able to claim your inner power and create the life you desire.

Will you claim this power? Or will you continue to defer responsibility to others for the choices you make?

*- Know Responsibility -*

Consider carefully, and know you are supported as you choose.

Over the coming months, more shall be revealed to you about your world and about the Universal Whole. Some of you will reject these messages, and that is as it needs be, for not all can hear at this time.

This does not mean that those of you who do hear and heed are "special" or "better." It means merely that some are ready while others are not; and that some hear some things, while others hear other things.

Your role may be to share what you hear, what you learn, but be mindful of pride and arrogance. Be mindful of insisting that you know the only truth; for what is true for you may not yet be true for others.

Be mindful of feeling superior over those who do not see what you see or have not learned what you have learned, for you are not superior. You are merely different, and these differences do not make you better or worse. They are simply the way of things.

Your knowing is valid. Within you is more understanding and wisdom than that for which you give yourself credit.

However, be mindful. Your knowing is valid, but you are not one who has access to all of the knowledge of the Universe. Share and trust what you know, but guard against arrogance and closed-mindedness. This is the "double-edged sword," so to speak, of being an infinite being contained within a finite form. Not all that you know is true and correct, but you have more knowledge of what is true and correct than you realize. Simultaneously, what you know to be true and correct may not be so for everyone, for some truth is subjective.

Share what you know when you feel called to do so, but

## - Know Responsibility -

respect and honor that others hold vast knowledge within themselves as well, and they are not required to heed what you say. Believing that you know more or know better than others is ego and hubris, and benefits no one.

With freedom comes responsibility. This is something of which most of you are cognizant, and yet you ignore or forget where your responsibility lies.

You have freedom to choose the actions you wish to take, but as you make these choices, know too that freedom to act comes with the acceptance of the consequences of your actions. Freedom to act does not mean you are free from consequences or results.

You may do as you choose. But if you are unwilling to accept that others might take issue with your choices, or that you may receive punishment for your choice, or that your actions might harm another, then you are not truly acting from freedom. You are acting from a desire to prove to everyone that you cannot be controlled. Yet in so doing, you are showing that you cannot control yourself, and it is only over yourself that control truly exists.

You are unable to be truly free if you are unwilling to be responsible for and within your freedom.

Many of you question at this time what the best course of action might be for yourself, your families, and the world as a whole.

The answer to one might not be the answer to all. You are free to choose the course of action you believe best for you, but you do not have the right to force that course upon any other. If you are parenting young children, you may choose the course you believe to be best for them, but it is not your place to dictate the course that is best for other parents' children.

*- Know Responsibility -*

When humans believe something strongly, they often endeavor to force those beliefs on others, and cannot understand why others would disagree. It is time for you to release the conviction that all must believe as you do.

Choose your own best course. Choose the best course for the children for whom you are directly responsible by virtue of being their parent. But release your perceived need to choose everyone's course. Allow others their own choices.

When someone causes you pain directly, it is their responsibility. They have chosen an action that has caused you pain.

But examine, too, where that pain comes from within you. Did they intend pain? Have you perhaps misunderstood or mistaken their actions?

Likewise, when you experience an emotional reaction to something you see or hear, whose responsibility is your reaction? If, for example, something you read on your computer causes you to feel pain or anger, is that the responsibility of the person who posted what you have read, or is it yours?

You are not responsible for the actions of others. However, you are responsible for your reactions. Choosing to allow your anger or pain to cause you to lash out or condemn someone for an action they took without knowledge of its effect on you--and perhaps without even knowing you--does not serve and does not solve the problem.

Examine your reactions and find the bounds of your responsibility. Choose to respond in ways that do not cause harm, particularly in cases where the other person meant no harm to you.

Some of you tend, out of anger or frustration, to attempt to control the actions of others. You attempt to take

*- Know Responsibility -*

responsibility for their actions and to urge or even manipulate them into acting as you wish.

At this time, I invite you to remember where your control and responsibility begin and end. You cannot force others to behave as you would like. You cannot control their behavior or choices.

Breathe. When another causes you frustration or disrupts something you are endeavoring to create or do, breathe. Remember that they are autonomous and will make their own choices; your choice is in how you respond.

You can change how you react and respond at these times. Consider how you might do so.

How is it that one can view the world and see only ugliness? Beloveds, so much beauty awaits you when you open your eyes, mind, and heart to it.

It seems to be human nature to comment upon the flaws and follies of others. Tend, rather, to the changes you know you need make to be prepared to truly aid others. Judgment does not come from another's actions, but from your observation of your own flaws, which are magnified in your own eyes because such is the nature of humans.

Address your own need to change rather than focusing upon what you believe others must alter about themselves. Judge only yourself, not harshly, but with an eye toward, "How might I change this? What might I alter to be the person I wish to be?"

You are not responsible for others. Only for yourself. Own and honor that responsibility.

When another speaks poorly of you, particularly in accusations or behind your back as it were, perhaps this is to be released. They do not create who you are, and many

## - Know Responsibility -

humans judge in others what they see within themselves rather than what is truly within those others.

However, if one comes to you and states that you have caused them pain or harm, it is not for you to refute them. While you may have done so unintentionally, if they state they experienced pain or harm due to your actions, this is true for them. If they seek communication and validation of their experience, it is not for you to tell them they are wrong.

This is not the same as when another levels accusations of general malice toward you. This is a case where one has come to discuss with you a specific situation in which you caused pain or harm. When this occurs, meet them with compassion and apologies. Take responsibility for what you have caused, even when it was not your intention. Respond to them as you would wish them to respond were the circumstances reversed. And know that inadvertently causing pain or harm does not negate the person you are, nor is it cause for guilt, merely for reflection, validation, and reconciliation when possible.

Among you, there are those who have become rigid and unwilling to relax beliefs and opinions to accommodate even hearing those of other people.

It is time to listen. To hear, even if you choose not to accept. To recognize that your way is not the only true way, even if it is the only way which is true for you.

In the Universe, there are many paths. There are many systems of belief. There are many beings who have formed their beliefs and code based upon their experiences. Experiences you might not share, and therefore do not recognize the validity of their system.

Know that your beliefs are valid unless they involve causing harm to yourself or others. Deliberately causing harm is never a valid path.

*- Know Responsibility -*

But just as your path is valid, so are the paths of others. If it does not bring harm, it is a valid path even should you disagree.

You do not need to agree with another's path to accept their right to follow that path. Open your mind to other possibilities, even those with which you do not agree or those you do not share. This is how you begin to heal your world.

## KNOW CHANGE

Prepare yourselves for that which is to come.

I do not warn you of impending "doom and gloom," as some may say. However, vast changes are approaching in your world and for some individuals in their lives. While it is not yet to be known what awaits on the other side of those changes, I encourage you to prepare for the changes themselves.

There is a word in Sanskrit which, in the language in which this message is written, translates roughly to "the pain which comes from change." Some may term this "growing pains," for growth is not merely physical.

Many of you may experience this type of pain as you progress over the coming weeks and months. Know that this is not a sign that things are going poorly, nor is it a sign of being on the wrong path, so to speak. It is merely indicative of the facet of human nature that resists change and fears the unknown.

Prepare to navigate this time. Gather your resources and know that you are not alone. You have support and love from those both seen and unseen, and as you allow yourselves to reach out to these people and beings for aid, so too shall you aid them. And all shall be well.

For some, now is a time of birth or rebirth.

Know that birth is not something which occurs only once. Each time you reach a new stage of your life, you may be said to be born into that next stage.

It is a time of endings, and after an ending comes a beginning. A new birth.

Be open to allowing things to end, for endings must come before beginnings. The way must be cleared for the new.

Be open to reaching out as you navigate this transition, for there is no shame in needing help, and you are not alone.

You are ready, or this time would not be presenting itself to you. Know this as you undergo the next step.

Prepare yourselves for change. In the coming weeks and months, many shifts will occur in your world. This is not, as some would say, "an awakening," nor is it exclusive to a chosen few. Change occurs frequently throughout creation, and all are part of it.

In the coming weeks and months, some of you may experience fear and discomfort. You may experience things which seem negative or painful.

Know that with change comes fear and pain, but this does not indicate that the changes are nonbeneficial. It indicates only that humans are conditioned to fear change and be hurt by it.

All shall be well in the fullness of time. Know this as you progress through the coming time. All shall be well.

At this time, you are called to prepare yourselves for what is to come in your world over the coming months. This is a

*- Know Change -*

time of change and reconfiguration. Not all will experience it in the same way, and this is as it need be, for one of the things that shall aid you and your world in healing and progressing is the recognition and validation of multiple paths and experiences.

Prepare yourselves for pain and fear, for these may occur. But prepare yourselves also to accept the wonder and abundance, the joy, that shall arise as you progress.

All may seem dark and lost at this time, but that is an illusion created by your fears and egos. All is never lost. At times it is simply necessary to work or seek more intentionally.

I assure you now that ultimately, all shall be well. However, you are invited to work to aid that coming time to reach fruition. Within yourselves, you hold the wisdom that might help guide your world. Will you accept and use it, or fall prey to conspiracies and falsehoods spread by those who seek accolades and acolytes?

Choose well and wisely.


At this time, you face the threshold of change, and your fear is growing. Stepping through that doorway, as it were, will bring you into the unknown, and for some of you, that is untenable.

You hesitate. That is acceptable. Feeling the fear is acceptable. Yet I encourage you to release the hold the fear has upon you. I encourage you now to choose to step across that threshold despite the fear.

You need not release the fear itself, nor need you stop feeling it; you may act despite it, and it is this which I encourage you to do.

Step despite fear. And know that all shall be well, even if what lies on the other side of the threshold is yet unknown to you.

*- Know Change -*

Some things in your lives are now coming to an end. This is not a negative experience, but merely part of the cycle which is part of all life.

Endings, however, can be painful. They can cause sadness and grief.

I encourage you to accept these changes and endings, but also to accept your emotions. Allow yourself to feel as you feel. Give yourself the gift of expressing those feelings in healthy, non-damaging ways. State how you feel to others in your life and allow them to state their feelings as well.

Endings are part of change, and these endings shall clear the way for positive new creations. But as things end, know that however you feel is acceptable.

Aspects of your life are coming to an end. Be ready for the changes which await you. But know also that you do not face these changes alone.

You are embraced. You are supported. You need only to reach out and accept the love and support which awaits you.

Reach out mindfully, for there are those, seen and unseen, who offer falsehoods. But know that there are those who have your highest benefit at heart, and it is to those you may reach out.

You are not alone. And benefit awaits you on the other side of change.

Before new creations can arise, the old must fall.

This is a difficult concept for some, for you view destruction as negative and harmful. I wish you to understand that not all destruction is negative. Just as in constructing a new building, an old one may be removed, so too must one remove certain aspects of life, certain factors, even certain

## - Know Change -

people in order to create a new, positive life.

Release your fears of destruction, for the endings and the falling of certain things in your life at this time is not negative. It is to clear the way for new abundance, new positives. Although some changes may be painful or frightening, know that ultimately, all shall be to your highest benefit.

Why do you struggle against change? Change is not the enemy, yet many of you treat it as though it is. When change comes, you rail and rant against it. You close your eyes to the possibilities and growth, and dig in your heels, as one might say, to avoid going forward. Yet you claim to be awakened. Beloveds, how can you awaken when you will not open your eyes?

Open your eyes now. Slowly. Take in the light. The colors. The beauty.

There is no fear here. Darkness, yes, for darkness and light have and always will coexist for as long as there has been day and night. Darkness is not the enemy any more than is change.

Some of you are awakening. Some do not know what that truly means. For now, know that it means seeing light and darkness equally, both as beautiful, both as necessary. Embrace them both, especially what dwells within each of you. And be ready for the work and change that lie ahead.

You are on the threshold of change. This is a prospect which both excites and frightens you.

Change is painful at times, and yet ultimately the changes you face will bring about positive lives and abundance for you. Face the changes which come with trust and belief in your own ability to withstand the storms and your own power to create the life you wish to live.

Be ready, in the coming days and weeks, for whatever

*- Know Change -*

comes to you, for all of it will bring about the changes you seek and need in order to improve your situation.

You are not alone in facing these changes. Reach out for support from your loved ones, your friends, your guides, any higher power in which you believe. Know that others are with you, seen or unseen.

Soon, in your world, a time shall come when many shifts and changes will occur simultaneously. Many of these will be to the benefit of your kind as a whole, yet some will cause strife. Some of these changes will be painful, even if beneficial, for change brings pain and discomfort until it is complete.

Be kind to yourselves as your world goes through this time, but be compassionate also toward others. Your way of managing the changes and addressing them is not everyone's way, and that is as it must be. Each of you knows what is right and best for you; none knows what is right and best for all.

Support one another through this time. Show kindness. Offer insight, but accept others' rejection of what you offer. You hold knowledge; so do they. At times, that knowledge may not match one another, and that, too, is as it must be.

Know that you--your people, your world--shall come through this time into a time of peace and abundance. All struggles shall not end, for that is not the way of things, but your world is likely to become a more peaceful, beneficial place if all work to support one another and show kindness and joy.

Energy shifts and changes constantly, yet often you are unaware of those shifts. Of late, however, the shifts have been so strong, so intense, that unawareness of them is nearly impossible.

Know that the shifts and changes you are experiencing at this time, though perhaps too intense or problematic for some, will ultimately settle out into a much more beneficial pattern. Some are experiencing sleep disruptions or illness at this time; those things shall come to an end shortly.

Your world is changing, and you are part of the change as you are part of the world. Bear with the changes, as you might say, and know that soon, all shall be well.

The world continues to turn. Seasons continue to change. The cycle of life, death, and birth continues to revolve. And yet you feel loss. You feel heavy. You feel as though nothing is right or will ever be the same.

Beloved, it is true that nothing will ever be the same, for nothing ever is. Change is inevitable and necessary. Even as the cycles continue, they are different each time. Life is not stagnant. Creation is not still. All does, and must, change.

However, your feeling of loss and grief is unnecessary. That is not to invalidate it, for your feelings and emotions are always valid, and you may feel however you feel. But there is no loss. There is only change, sometimes painful, sometimes beautiful, always needed.

I speak not of loss of loved ones, for that is pain, and whatever occurs beyond death is not for you to know. Grieve those you have lost as you need to grieve. This is not the loss of which I speak.

I speak of your feelings of loss of "normalcy," of "the usual way." These things are not lost, they are simply transmuting and evolving.

Mourn what you need to mourn. Grieve what you need to grieve. But know that all shall be well.

Your world is changing. This has been stated previously, and continues to be the case, for change is one of the only true constants in the Universe.

*- Know Change -*

Your world is changing, and you have the choice of whether to change with it. Know that you are not alone in this choice. All beings, from time to time, reach a point when they must choose whether to continue to grow and progress, or whether to dig in their heels, as it were, and stagnate.

Your world is changing, and it will change with or without you. It will change whether or not you accept the changes.

Become willing to change. Know that change is at times uncomfortable, but it is ultimately beneficial, and it is necessary for existence.

Become willing to reach out for assistance when change becomes too frightening or overwhelming.

Be willing, above all, to accept that you are not alone, and that you are capable of growth and abundance.


Your world seems to be swirling ever faster. In chaos. In fear and destruction.

Know that this destruction is needed. One cannot build when a structure already stands. One cannot create where other creations take up the space.

The destruction you see now is causing harm and damage. Of that there can be no doubt. It is perfectly valid and acceptable to feel sadness, anger, and other "negative" emotions. Those who observe your world experience some of the same.

Under the anger and fear, however, may you feel hope and safety. Your world may not be a safe place now, but it will become so in your lifetime. The changes have already begun. The winds are shifting, as it were, and blowing away that which harms and does not serve. New building, new growth, is coming.

Be part of that growth. Be ready to embrace it, for it will bring your world a time the likes of which you have not seen.

*- Know Change -*

These sound like platitudes meant to calm a child. I assure you this is the future that is at the highest probability at this time. Futures may be altered, however, so be mindful of the actions you take, and endeavor to help this future come to pass.

As this world spins ever closer to a large shift in energies and perceptions, some of you are feeling the sensations of pain and discomfort. Know that this is normal. Humans are conditioned to shy away from change and alteration in their "normal," and this change shall be vaster than you may understand.

Know that the time shall come when your world reaches the next stage, and that you, as you read this, are part of that change. You are one to guide others through their pain and discomfort. But be mindful of doing so at the expense of your own needs and comfort.

You are not meant to be a grandiose leader, but a quiet guide, one who may not receive accolades and praise but will see the fruits of your efforts. Offer aid and comfort for the sake of those you help rather than for the sake of what you might gain. This does not mean you may not seek recompense if so moved and so warranted; you are allowed some gain. But these gains shall not include your name shouted from the rooftops.

If you seek fame, you have chosen a path which will lead you away from that. However, fame is not the reason to assist your world in shifting. Know your true reason.

As changes begin to occur with increasing rapidity in your lives, I encourage you to seek aid when you need it. This may be a time of upheaval and confusion for you, and there is no need to face it alone.

You may seek support from friends and loved ones. From

*- Know Change -*

your guides, Even from professionals, for this is no shame or harm in seeking the support of those who are trained to give it.

This is not a time to face things on your own, for at times, many of us, even those who are not human, require support and assistance from others. None of us exists in isolation. All are part of the Whole of the Universe.

The changes which are to come shall be beneficial, but this does not mean they shall be easy. When difficulties arise, when pain comes to you, reach out. You are not alone.

Change is cause for both celebration and fear. Celebration, for it brings about the end of difficulties and opens the way for more positive times; fear because it is unknown what awaits on the other side of change.

All that you feel in response to change is valid. Your emotions are valid and will not impede the change from occurring. Nor will negative emotions prevent the occurrence of positive events, although some teach that this is so.

Be mindful of your thoughts and actions as you proceed through times of change, for what you think, say, and do has an impact. However, know too that you have the ultimate choice of how you think, speak, and act.

All shall be well. Trust that this is so.

Know that while there are shifts and changes occurring within your world, not every negative thing which occurs is a sign of change. Some are, rather, signs of things which need to be changed, or of things which will endure and with which you must find peace and a means of survival.

Many seek explanations for things which simply cannot be explained and reject or even demonize those who believe differently. Hatred is not a sign that your world is "evolving,"

*- Know Change -*

but rather something out of which the world needs to evolve.

This is the time to awaken. Awaken to your own power, to what you are able to control, to the things for which you are responsible. This is the time to claim that power and take that responsibility. Sitting back and stating, "We are awakening, everything will be fine if you reject everything except light and love" will not bring about the change, growth, and healing for which you hope. Rather, they will only cover up the darkness, and that will allow negatives to continue to flourish.

It is a time of awakening, but the awakening which must occur is within each of you and is individual and unique to each person. You can determine only your own awakening, your own growth and evolution. Will you accept this task?

## KNOW BALANCE

Stand in the sunlight today, beloveds. Stand in the light of truth and of knowing. Seek the light within yourselves and within one another, for it is present within nearly all of you.

But recognize, too, the darkness. Know that darkness is a necessary balance to light, but know also that some have chosen to embrace and live solely in darkness.

Light does not conquer darkness, nor does it seek to do so. Instead, light seeks a balance with darkness. Light and darkness seek to honor one another and create balance in the Universe. Those who have chosen to embrace only light are, in some ways, no more benevolent than those who have chosen to embrace only darkness.

Seek balance. As you stand in the light today, honor it, but honor, too, the shadow, the darkness, for without one, the other cannot exist.

Beauty lives all around you, yet some choose to see only ugliness. Beauty dwells within you, yet some choose to see only their own ugliness and darkness.

## - Know Balance -

Beloveds, darkness is beauty as much as is light. You were created, as were all beings, with both qualities. There is no need to seek to eliminate darkness, but only to learn to manage it. To see it for its beauty and lessons rather than allowing it to become ugly and to control your interactions with others.

Some of you speak of "shadow work," and this is akin to what I mean. In this work, one learns to embrace their "shadows," their darkness, and honor and acknowledge it while teaching it to be productive and beneficial.

This is what you are called on to do. Embrace all aspects of yourself, for all are needed. Honor those hidden places within you that were told to cease existence. Heal these parts, and you will heal not only yourself, but the world.

Each year, at a certain time, your world enters a time of darkness. A time when the hours of darkness outweigh the hours of light.

Each year, after several months, your world enters a time of light. A time when the hours of light outweigh the hours of darkness.

This is a cycle which exists year after year, millennium after millennium. It is part of the natural order of things. At times, darkness outweighs light. At times, light outweighs darkness. You see this and accept it as the natural cycle and balance of things.

Why, then, do you reject the balance of light and darkness within yourselves? Why, when the entire world consists of a balance between light and darkness, do you believe you must eliminate the darkness within yourself and exist as purely light?

Not only is this inaccurate, it is impossible. Light cannot exist without darkness. Darkness cannot exist without light. And a balanced world cannot exist without a balance between the two.

Learn to embrace both aspects of yourself. To understand that both have their place and role, and both are beneficial in their ways.

Cease seeking to eliminate half of yourself. Existing purely as "light" is no more desirable nor beneficial than existing as purely "darkness."

Learn to exist in balance. Learn to embrace that balance within you.

In times of darkness, whether literal or figurative, I invite you to remember that light, too, exists. Darkness is not the enemy. It is merely one part of the balance of the Universal Whole.

Release fear of the darkness both outside you and within you. Learn to embrace darkness as a time or a sign of rest and resetting. Just as animals hibernate at times, sometimes darkness in your world is a sign that you would benefit from hibernating, from allowing yourself to retreat and rest. To restore yourself on an energetic, emotional, and physical level.

Darkness is not synonymous with evil or negativity, though many humans use it as such. Darkness is merely part of the necessary balance of things. Honor it as part of this balance, part of the cycling of seasons and of life. Learn to work with it rather than against it.

Look around you. See the light and the shadow. See both and know that both are necessary for the existence of the Universe.

Some of you reject the shadows within yourselves and others. This does not serve you. Just as both must exist for the balance of the Universe to be maintained, so must both exist for each individual to be in balance.

- *Know Balance* -

The danger comes not from the existence of the shadow, but from the denial of it. The rejection of it.

Seek not to deny or eliminate the shadows, but rather to incorporate them into your balance. This is a path to healing.

As you move through your life, strive to accept balance between what you know and what you learn. Between light and darkness. Between your beliefs and the beliefs of others.

Your world is fractured and damaged, yet this damage, this illness as it were, is correctable, if humans choose to work in balance with themselves, each other, and the Universe as a Whole.

Connect again with nature. With other people. With the beings who exist to work with you. Seek connections among the human world and the world of nature. Seek connections among the various parts of yourself.

To heal the world, it is first necessary to heal yourself. This does not mean one must be "fully healed" to effect change, but merely that one must recognize the pieces within themself that are in need of healing and begin that work.

When you heal yourself, as you work toward healing, you do heal the world, for all is interconnected.

Your world is fractured. It is time for the healing to begin. Will you choose to contribute to it?

Balance is a necessary quality of the Universe as well as of individuals. Yet some humans, in the name of "enlightenment" or "spirituality," reject balance and proclaim that only goodness, only light, should exist.

It is human nature to fear the darkness. To fear the negative aspects of oneself. But seeking to eliminate those things is no more beneficial than seeking to eliminate goodness and light.

## - Know Balance -

Balance, beloveds. Balance is what is needed to truly create a beneficial world for yourselves and others. The teaching that only light should exist is a false teaching created by ego, for just as both day and night must exist, so must both light and darkness.

I ask you to seek balance, not rejection. We, the beings who seek to work with and support you, encourage you to find the true balance, and to refrain from condemning others for accepting that both light and darkness exist.

Within each of you, there is light. As well, there is darkness.

It is true and well that both exist. Balance is the most necessary quality in the Universe. Without darkness, there cannot be light.

The darkness within you is the stillness. It is the pain. It is the qualities which do not serve you, but also the qualities which serve only you.

The light within you is the accomplishments. The aid and solace you offer to others. The qualities which serve others as well as you.

All aspects of you are part of who you are, just as all aspects of the Universal Whole are what the Universe is. Seek, then, not to eliminate any of your aspects, but to learn to work with them, to change, perhaps, how you approach them or allow them to manifest. But honor and acknowledge all of them as part of you, for you are worthy of honor and acknowledgement.

For some of you, now is a time for facing your own darkness. Your "shadow self," as some term it.

As you progress in this work, be mindful of identifying yourself as your shadow, rather than identifying the shadow as

*- Know Balance -*

part of your Self.

You are not the darkness. You are, rather, a perfect, harmonious balance of darkness and light, as is all Creation. This is something you have forgotten or of which you have lost sight, but it is true. The work of this time is to reclaim that harmony, that balance; it is not to eliminate the darkness or shadow, but to incorporate it and claim it as part of you.

But at the same time, light is part of you as well. You are not the shadow, not the light; you are both, in a complete, glorious whole that mirrors the Whole of Creation.

This is the work you are called to. Recognizing, incorporating, and honoring all aspects of yourself, while knowing that you are not the aspects but rather are the whole.

## KNOW CONNECTION

In your world, disconnection is a theme. It is something which has become prized and valued, and yet disconnection is the cause of so much of the struggle and illness in your world.

I speak not only of disconnection from others, but from yourself. You have become accustomed to listening to the professionals and to the self-proclaimed "gurus" and healers of your time.

While they may hold knowledge that can benefit you, when you heed them at the cost of connecting to and listening to yourself, you do yourself a disservice. You cause yourself pain and perhaps illness which would otherwise not be present.

Spend time each day, even a moment or two, in silence connecting with yourself. With your body. With your mind. With your energy.

Restore the innate connections which you have, however unwittingly, severed in the course of living a "normal" life.

Connection is key to healing. Restore and rebuild these and see how things change for you.

*- Know Connection -*

Your world today is divided. For some, your nation is divided. And yet the great Whole of which all beings are a part is still there.

Take a moment today to reflect upon that Whole. That love. That connection. Reflect upon your place in it.

Honor those who were lost, but also those who remain. Honor the Whole. Honor love. And know that the same connection and compassion can be created anew, without such extremes as in the past.

What step can you take to help with this creation today?

It is a tendency for some of you to withdraw. To curl up, as it were, into your individuality and deny that you are part of a larger whole.

I ask that you remember that you are part of that Whole. You may withdraw as you need, for all actions are subject to the choice and will of the one who acts. Yet know that even when you withdraw, even when you deny, yet you are still part of this Whole.

For some, this is an overwhelming thought. It is larger than your mind can comfortably comprehend. That is all right. You need not comprehend it all for it to be true.

We are with you. Your guides are with you. The beings who work with humans, and other humans, are with you. When you are ready to emerge from your cocoon, still we shall be with you, waiting to welcome you as part of the Whole.

Now, perhaps more than at any other time in human history, it is time for you to connect. It is time for you to reach out to one another and aid each other in navigating the challenges which face you as individuals and as a world.

However, some refuse to connect. Some refuse to believe

## - Know Connection -

that another's struggles are not the "fault" of that person. Some tend only to themselves and show no care or compassion.

To progress through the current challenges and reach the next stage, connection and compassion are imperative. None of you exists in isolation. You are all part of the world, and all part of the Whole. When one falls behind, all lag.

Determine how you might connect with and aid others while tending also to your own growth. Determine how you may reach out for connection and support for yourself.

Know that you are not alone. Not as individuals and not as a world. Refusing connection serves no one.

How shall you begin to rebuild your world? This is a question in the minds of many, and yet some believe the rebuilding is the responsibility of "someone else."

Who is that "someone"? Who, if not each of you?

Each human has a role to play in the growth and change of the world as a whole. Each of you shall contribute, though the ways in which you contribute may be so small as to be unnoticeable to you and others.

Know, however, that each thing you do to endeavor to improve your world has an effect, and these effects ripple as water in a pond. Your seemingly miniscule actions will create great change if you refrain from fear and release the resistance to acting at all.

You will create change, beloveds. Know this to be true.

Listen to the wind. To the trees. To running water. To the sounds of nature around you.

You have become disconnected from the natural world, and yet nature is an integral part of your world. Without nature, humankind cannot exist. And without humankind,

*- Know Connection -*

nature may suffer, though sadly it suffers in the presence of humans as well.

It is time to cease living a life of isolation and self-containment. It is time to recognize and restore your connection with the world around you. With the wonderment of nature and all it holds.

Take this time.

Attune to your surroundings. Truly feel into how it is to be where you are. This includes both your manmade surroundings and those created by Nature, for you are part of all of it.

Attune to these things, while refraining from allowing yourself to identify as these things. If you are in surroundings which do not please you, or which cause you to feel negatively, remember that you are not your location any more than you are your past or the people with whom you dwell.

Yet attuning to what is around you will not only allow you a sense of connection, it will begin to change those things. All is affected by all else. Your energy, your spirit, as it were, will affect your surroundings just as they affect you.

Attune and connect, and yet retain your sense of self and know that this brings benefit to what is around you.

Today, let yourself walk in the light. I do not say this figuratively, but mean the literal light of the Sun. Exit your home if it is safe to do so. Even in clouds and rain, the Sun is there to shine upon you.

Take in this light, this warmth, this beauty. Allow yourself to bathe in it, even to wallow, for you have shut yourself away from light for too long. Bask in it and do so with full intention and mindfulness.

Many things which you have taken for granted have been

*- Know Connection -*

removed from your life. The Sun is still there, and some still take it for granted.

Honor it today, and in so doing, honor yourself, for the same being which created the Sun created you.

Place yourself in nature. In the world you have forsaken for the pleasures of electronics and the comfort of indoors.

You are losing your connection with the natural world, and this is one reason humans struggle so mightily at this time. Rather than seeing yourselves as interconnected with one another and the world as a whole, you see yourself as individuals who have no need of or desire for connection with any.

You see yourselves as sole proprietors of what is and what is not. Of what is necessary and unneeded. You see yourselves as the only ones who matter.

This is what causes the strife in your world. This sense, this belief, that there is no connection.

Place yourself in the world. Place yourself among humans, among animals, among plants. Amongst all of it, you belong, and you are connected whether you wish to see it or not.

Your actions affect far more than yourself. Would you wish others to treat you as you choose to treat life?

Consider your place in the interwoven tapestry of Life. And create the place you wish to hold.

Of late, many of you have been required to remain in your homes. Going outside has become a thing filled with fears and danger.

However, through this requirement, you have begun to lose your connection with nature and the world.

Restore that connection as much as you are able. Even setting foot outside the door of your home onto a small patch

*- Know Connection -*

of grass, or standing near a tree growing through the sidewalk, will soothe you and bring you back toward balance.

Nature exists as a gift to bring you peace in times when peace seems impossible to find. This is one such time. I encourage you to step outside, if only for a moment. Breathe the air if no other forms of nature exist within reach. Connect. Feel yourself as part of something larger than the current situation could ever be.

Each small action you take affects more than you may realize. You are not an isolated speck in the fabric of the Universe, but a part of a glorious interwoven Whole. Small actions, even small thoughts, can have a broad effect.

How, then, shall you choose to affect the Universe? How shall you contribute to the Whole?

Meditate upon these questions and listen to the answers you receive. Feel yourself as part of something greater, rather than feeling the loneliness and isolation which often plague you.

Feel, know, and trust your place in the Whole. And know that you are as vital as any.

Soon in your world there will come a time when you will have the power to create great change. While your role may seem small, know that each action you choose, each word you speak, ripples outward beyond the bounds of what you can see.

Know that your choices make a difference. You, even if you feel small and insignificant, make a difference.

Do that which you feel most called to do and know that it will contribute to the changes which are coming to your world.

*- Know Connection -*

In your life, there have been those who have aided and supported you but then have left your life.

Know that these people may not have been intended to remain in your life forever. Each of you has a path. At times, those paths converge and you may walk together for a time, but then the paths diverge once again, and you must part.

Their absence from your life is not personal. It is not something you have done wrong. It is merely that their path has diverged from yours.

Rather than railing against them for abandoning you, or resenting them for no longer being present, strive to find joy in the time you had together. Look for the gifts and gains those times brought you and be content in the memories rather than angry at the lack of time together in the present.

When you bemoan the loss of friendships or connections, when you comment upon the lack of communication from others, ask whether you are engaging in the same behaviors.

Have you reached out to these people? Have you been in communication with them?

Connection is, as you may say, a two-way street. There is no single person who is responsible for contact and communication in an interaction between two people.

You need not be the only one to reach out; and if this is the case for you, you may choose to end the connection. But you also need not wait for another to reach out to you if you have not made similar overtures.

Connection is reciprocal. Examine your side of the connection and determine what you are contributing to maintaining it.

Rise from your bed or chair. Go to the window.

What do you see outside the glass? Take a moment to

*- Know Connection -*

observe each person and thing within sight.

Take a moment to truly *feel* these people and things. To recognize them as pieces of the infinite Whole.

Feel yourself as part of this Whole also. You who isolate yourself. You who shun the company of others. You who believe yourself to be above it all. Feel yourself as part of the infinite Whole.

No human is isolated. No one exists in a vacuum, as it were. Each of you has a place and a role within the infinite.

One need not be, as you may say, a "social butterfly," or accept and agree with all people, in order to allow connection with the Universe. Each has their place in the infinite.

Feel this. Revel in it.

Among you, there are many differences. At times, those differences rouse fear and hatred. This is a sad state, for few differences render anyone undeserving of love and respect.

See your fellow humans as creations of the Universe, just as you yourself are. I speak not of those who deliberately harm others, for this is a difference which need not be accepted. But differences among race, or ethnicity, or religion, or the myriad other criteria by which humans judge and reject one another, are not measures of who anyone is.

Seek to accept others as you wish acceptance for yourself. You need not like each individual you meet, but seek to learn not to reject entire groups of people solely because you do not agree with or understand who they are.

Of late, there has seemed a tendency for humans to judge one another's experiences and dismiss those experiences which do not match their own.

This is harmful and even damaging to others. No two people--no two beings of any type--experience or perceive everything in exactly the same manner. One person may experience severe trauma from something which merely causes another a minor inconvenience. One person may communicate with beings they identify as angels, while another communicates with beings of light. One may heal from their trauma through discussing it and connecting with others who have experienced trauma, while another copes with their trauma by refusing to speak of it.

Your ways are valid as long as they cause no harm to yourself or others. But others' ways are equally valid as long as they cause no harm.

Refrain from judging and negating others' experiences because they are not your own. Accept and honor that all beings have unique perspectives and perceptions, and that all of these are true for the individuals who have them.

Each of you has a place in the Universe. In the world. Most importantly, in your own life.

Sometimes as humans you lose sight of your place. You believe you have no place, no right to exist. You believe that you do not fit or belong.

I tell you that this is an illusion. Each of you is part of the glorious Whole that comprises the Universe. Were you to not exist, the Universe would not be as it is. You are integral, even should you be unaware of this.

Recognize your place. Recognize that you are needed.

You are not alone.

You have never been alone.

You have lost sight of or lost connection to those around you, but this is an illusion. Those connections have never truly gone. The connections to those who have caused you harm or pain may have dissolved or been removed, and this is well for

*- Know Connection -*

you; you need not maintain connection to those who have harmed you.

But surrounding you are your guides. Other beings who wish to assist you. Your ancestors and those yet to come into your world. Souls and spirits with whom you have lived other lives or will live other lives, for in some realms, time is not a linear thing.

When you feel most isolated and alone, reach out to those who are with you or connected to you. Seek those who are truly with you for your benefit, for at times entities will attempt to delude you into believing they are benevolent when they are not. But you will know the truth within yourselves. Ask for your own guides, for your ancestors, for the deities with whom you work if this is your path.

Feel your connections to the Whole of Creation and know that you are never truly alone.

## SHIVA'S CLOSING MESSAGE

It is my hope that through the words on the pages of this book, you shall find hope, healing, and guidance as you progress along your life's path.

It is my hope equally that you shall use your own intuition and discernment to determine which messages resonate for you and which do not, for not all messages are meant for all readers.

Your life is your own. Some of you have lost sight of this fact, so I remind you again: Your life is your own. Only you have the power and the right to determine the direction that life will take. You, and you alone, are the one to decide how and whether to heal, to learn, to grow.

These messages, and others I and my Ganatram share, are not intended as commands or directives, but as nudges, so to speak. As topics to ponder, things to consider, as you formulate your path.

We are honored to have walked with you along the small part of your journey that has included reading this book. I am pleased to have been able to share with you the perspective

## - Shiva's Closing Message -

and knowledge I have gained in my existence, and I hope it benefits you.

You are never alone. Call upon me. Upon your own guides. Although you may not be connected with them as yet, they are there. Future materials will be made available to you that will facilitate your safe connection with these beings who exist in part to aid and guide you; in the meantime, know simply that they are there, and they wish the best for you.

I appreciate your time reading the words in these pages, and I hope they will bring you peace and wisdom—both wisdom from without and from within—for the next stage of your journey.

Be well and be loved.

*- Acknowledgements -*

## ACKNOWLEDGEMENTS

To the readers, thank you for purchasing this book. I hope the messages Shiva has offered are as helpful and reassuring to you as they are to me, and that they give you a sense of support and compassion in your life journey. The messages are intended to help you on your path, whatever that might be, and I hope they serve to do so.

Channeling is a gift I've had since childhood, and a skill I've practiced since 2006. I am grateful for the opportunity to bring Shiva's guidance and wisdom to others, and to those who have allowed me to share with them. It means a lot to be able to offer this to you.

I want to thank my mentor, Christopher, who taught me about guides and channeling so many years ago. Although the connection has long been severed and he's unlikely to ever read this, the knowledge and skills I learned from him have formed the cornerstone of my practice and of who I've become in the years since.

I thank Shiva and my other guides for having helped me through the worst times of my life, as well as being with me

## Acknowledgements

through the best. As a young child with no siblings and few friends, having my guides helped me feel as if I mattered to someone. In my teen years and at times in adulthood, these amazing beings helped me survive. I am honored by their willingness to work with me and support me even when I'm oppositional, and by Shiva's willingness to allow me to share his words with the world.

To my children Phoenix and Michaela, and my son-in-law Eric, thank you for supporting me and accepting me talking to you about all this "woo stuff." Particularly to Phoenix for having been one of the first recipients of a channeling session with Shiva so many years ago.

To my husband Steve, thank you for believing in me, even when you don't believe in the things I do.

To Elizabeth Silver, I greatly appreciate your formatting work and the belief in this book that led you to offer it. Thank you!

To Lex Valentine, thank you for working with me to create a cover that fits the energy of this book and persuading me that the colors I first chose wouldn't quite work. This one is so much better!

There are so many other people I want to thank, who have helped me with both my business and inner work, and I know I would leave someone out if I tried to name you all. (Wibbly-wobbly memory-wemory...) So I'll just say a ginormous thank you to all of you here; I hope you know who you are.

And to all those who have received channeling sessions with Shiva and me, thank you for your support, for your trust, and for the opportunities to work with you and continue building my skills. May your paths be smooth.

## ABOUT THE (HUMAN) AUTHOR

River Lightbearer (they/them) has been on a healing journey most of their adult life and has a passion for helping others heal and find their inner light. As a survivor of abuse and trauma, their heart is in guiding other survivors to gain ground in their journeys and create the lives they want to live. Their compassion, calming energy, and skills with the modality have supported numerous clients in their healing journeys.

Through their practice, River offers channeling and Chios® Energy Healing, both with a "side order" of mindset coaching, online/by distance to clients around the world.

River is a nonbinary eclectic Witch. In addition to this and other books under the River Lightbearer name, they also write or have written under the names Karenna Colcroft, KC Winter, Jo Ramsey, Kimberly Ramsey, and Kim Ramsey-Winkler. They are the mother to two nonbinary offspring and a son-in-law, as well as the grandmother to four wonderful children. River lives in Massachusetts with their husband. When not writing or serving other humans, River is the servant to two cats.

Learn more at https://riverlightbearer.com

## RIVEREVOLUTIONS

    RiverEvolutions is the name given to me to use in my practice as catalyst, channel, and healing practitioner, a reflection of my spiritual name, River Lightbearer. Through my work, I help survivors of trauma, as well as others, gain clarity and direction to progress on their healing journeys and throughout their lives.

    Channeling is the cornerstone of RiverEvolutions. In a channeling session, you're able to speak, directly or relayed through me, with one of my guides: Shiva, the being of light who worked with me to create this book, or Pietkela, a higher-level being who is transitioning with me to become the being with whom I work most closely. They share their profound wisdom and compassion to offer guidance and help you identify aspects of your life in which change would benefit you as well as aspects that benefit you now.

    Chios® Energy Healing, a method of working with your energy to bring positive changes to your mind and body, restores balance and flow to your energy system, bringing you clarity, calmness, and a heightened sense of well-being. I am a Certified Chios® Master Teacher and Chios® Master of Healing Consciousness.

Mindset coaching, which is a part of every session of any type with River, helps you identify thought and behavior patterns that keep you from the life you want to live, as well as helping you recognize the roots of those patterns and how you might change them.

For those who operate their own spiritually-based practices, I offer channeling sessions focused on your business and how best to proceed. For those seeking an additional service to add to your practice, I provide instruction in channeling and in the Chios® Energy Healing modality.

Learn more about me and my services by visiting http://www.riverevolutions.com or emailing info@riverevolutions.com.

www.ingramcontent.com/pod-product-compliance
Lightning Source LLC
Chambersburg PA
CBHW060819050426
42449CB00008B/1736